NEIL KINNOCK

NEIL KINNOCK

The Path to Leadership

G.M.F. DROWER

Weidenfeld and Nicolson
London

First published in Great Britain by
George Weidenfeld & Nicolson Limited
91 Clapham High Street, London SW4 7TA

Copyright © G.M.F. Drower, 1984

Cased ISBN 0 297 78467 6
Paperback ISBN 0 297 78522 2

Printed and bound in Great Britain by
Butler & Tanner Ltd, Frome and London

To Linda

Contents

Illustrations

Acknowledgements

The author is grateful to Neil Kinnock for granting him an interview and his office for providing some papers which have been helpful in writing this book. Thanks also to Dorothy Kinnock, Chris Mullin, Emlyn Williams, Mrs Joy Drower, Father George Brown OSB, Lord Teviot, Venetia Pollock, Duncan McNair, Dr Paul Taylor, Peter Hain, Anne McSherry-Alton, Robin Cook and Dr Diana Green. The information for this work was researched mainly from interviewing Neil Kinnock and from newspapers, written archives, *Hansard* and Labour Party Conference reports. Thanks are due to the broadcasting unit, library and press cuttings service at Labour Party Headquarters, Walworth Road; also to the London School of Economics Library, ITN, BBC, London Welsh Rugby Club, the Workers' Educational Association, the National Library of Wales, the National Union of Teachers, and the University of Cardiff Students Union.

Introduction

Neil Kinnock was elected leader of the Labour Party in autumn 1983. With the gradual decline of Labour in terms of electoral popularity since the time of Attlee, it seemed surprising at first that Labour should choose as its leader an unknown MP with no experience of government office. However, Kinnock's unsurpassed loyalty to the Labour Party has won him great affection among the trade unions and constituencies.

Kinnock's career has been one of the most spectacular in British political history. His considerable good fortune depends on two main factors: his Bevanite origins are appropriate to the mood of the broad left, who have triumphed during Labour's recent civil war; and the Party, after years of an apparently elderly and tentative leadership, needed a leader with a dynamic and tough young image.

What is generally not appreciated is that despite his appeals, as leader, for Party unity, Kinnock spent much of his career as an MP rebelling against the governments of Wilson and Callaghan. His defiance of the Labour government's plans for Welsh devolution showed greater integrity and personal and political courage than he is often given credit for. It showed, as did his shift of emphasis concerning the EEC, that Kinnock could be sufficiently pragmatic to alter left-wing policies.

Despite Kinnock's undoubtedly pleasant personality, there must be scepticism as to whether his jovial image will be adequate for Labour's needs. It is, arguably, a fatal underestimation of the intelligence of the British electorate to assume that Kinnock's verbosity will be sufficient to win Labour a general election. There is, moreover, little that is relevant to the contemporary British electorate in the Bevanite ideas of class, unilateral nuclear disarmament and the trade unions which he so reveres. There does also seem to be some mythology concerning Kinnock's ability as a vote winner. Despite his loyalty and determination to secure a Labour victory, Kinnock himself contributed to Labour's 1983 general election defeat. His Falklands speeches concerning the *Belgrano* and 'guts at Goose Green' lost sympathy. As shadow Education Secretary, his policies were rejected even by traditional Labour voters, such as teachers and the unemployed.

Were Mrs Thatcher to leave the political scene, the picture for Labour would change dramatically. By the time of a general election in 1988, Thatcher would have spent thirteen years as leader of the Conservative Party, and nine continuous years at the gruelling job of Prime Minister, thus overtaking Harold Wilson's record of being the longest serving peacetime Prime Minister since Gladstone. With the absence of a worthy successor since the demise of Francis Pym and Cecil Parkinson, the Conservatives might find that a general election fought with a leader other than Mrs Thatcher would lead to Kinnock securing a Labour victory.

Thus the picture for Labour's new leader is by no means bleak. If there is scepticism concerning Labour's ability to win a general election, it must be because of its obsolete policies. Were Labour to fail it would not be because of Kinnock's personality, for his wit, humour and charm have made him the most pleasant character in the modern British political scene.

local pit. In 1931, during the depression, the mines were closed and, rather than receive 10s. 6d. a week dole money, Gordon took a temporary job building the Tredegar swimming baths, on a public works programme. Four of his brothers could not get work and had to leave South Wales, never to return. It was an economic tragedy which fractured the family.

South Wales suffered badly during the depression; there was a universal hatred of the mine owners and the haughty conservative middle classes who, it was believed, had no idea what poverty meant. Such was the mood at the time that the local Tredegar council occasionally sent Stalin telegrams of congratulation. The miseries of life reinforced the belief that the working classes should stand firm with the trade unions. Archie Kinnock and his eldest sons took part in the General Strike, and the bitter memories of that terrible year made it a family tradition never to buy a comic published by a firm that had refused to recognize the trade unions. Gordon Kinnock would never allow such comics in the house. This solidarity with the trade unions was passed on, and when in 1978, fifty years later, Glenys Kinnock accidently sent Christmas cards with a picture from a comic – bought in Llandudno – Neil's friends were shocked. Neil issued his apologies, and new cards were sent.

At the time of the Second World War, Gordon Kinnock was conscripted to work in the mines. In December 1940 he married a hospital nurse, Mary Howells, at the Ebenezer Independence Chapel in the village of Aberdare, where Mary had been born thirty years earlier. Her father, William Howells, had been a miner at the Llewellyn colliery. When Mr Llewellyn was standing for election, at the constituency of Merthyr Boroughs, against the Labour leader, Keir Hardie, he asked each of his employees at the pithead how they were going to vote. Howells told him he wasn't going to vote for him and was dismissed a week later. Neil Kinnock's mother was a formidable woman of great determination and energy. She has often been described as ambitious, but Kinnock denies this. Instead he states that her concern was with 'personal serenity, very strong family duty, and cultural enjoyment, which to her meant mainly music'. A favourite phrase of hers, which she used often, stressed the need to be 'a good citizen'. Both parents loved music, and Gordon in his spare time was a clarinettist in a local jazz band known as the River Row Centurions. He also enjoyed soccer and rugby football. Despite little formal education, the Kinnocks were intelligent and widely read. During Mary's pregnancy, she and Gordon took lodgings at 1 Vale View, Tredegar, a small neat terraced house. Mrs Gertrude Padfield, who let the rooms to the young couple while her husband was serving overseas with the Army Education Corps, remembers Gordon Kinnock pacing about the house on 28 March 1942, awaiting the cries of the new baby. Mrs Padfield claims that the future leader of the Labour Party 'had a good voice even then'. The parents had not thought what to name the newborn child. Mrs Padfield suggested that, as they had a Scottish name, they should call him Neil. The parents agreed and the child was named Neil Gordon Kinnock.

In 1945 Gordon Kinnock developed dermatitis, a skin disease, on his hands and as a result was forced to leave mining. Although he had worked for nearly a quarter of a century in the mines, he received no compensation as dermatitis was not considered to be an industrial disease. The following year he found employment at the Ebbw Vale steelworks, where his job was to remove the lining from the buckets that carried the molten metal and then to reline, with firebricks, the furnaces which had been shut down. Gordon worked at Ebbw Vale until his death in 1971. Neil Kinnock remembers how each morning, before going to work, his father would have to have his hands wrapped in bandages because of dermatitis: 'My father, my grandfather, my uncles have all suffered from various industrial injuries and diseases.'

When Neil was born, Gordon and Mary decided to have no more children but to concentrate instead on giving their only son the opportunities in life that they had missed. Mary returned to nursing as soon as she possibly could, determined that her son would eventually gain the qualifications necessary for him to have a secure, physically safe job.

As Neil grew up, he proved to be a well-balanced, honest child who liked to make people laugh. He had a typical working-class childhood, and was sent to the local Tredegar Junior School. He was of average intelligence, but made very little effort, and is best remembered for his sense of humour. He was good at arts subjects, but no matter how much he was coached, he was poor at maths.

Neil was seldom indoors, but spent his time with his friends at football, rugby, and cricket. Like his father, he was very keen on sport, and early on was able to remember the names of all the Welsh teams, their scores and the matches they had won. Neil would often visit his Aunt Dorothy at Vale Terrace. She remembers him as a humorous but sensible child who well understood his father's and grandfather's constant reiteration to stand by his responsibilities. The young Kinnock loved to entertain an audience and developed a talent for mimicry which produced roars of laughter from his family. On occasions he would show signs of a terrible temper, but was soon laughing and joking again; one of his greatest strengths was an ability to laugh at himself. When he was nine years old his Aunt Dorothy asked him what he wanted to be when he grew up, and the future leader of the Labour Party said, to much family amusement, that he wanted to be a private detective.

The South Wales environment of Kinnock's youth was to have a great effect on his political thinking. As Mary Kinnock now had the job of Tredegar's district nurse, during the school vacations she would take her son with her on her rounds visiting the sick. Nurse Kinnock was popular, and much loved in Tredegar: she knew the local families but never indulged in gossip. Neil remembers seeing the suffering of the old and the ill on these visits; it left an indelible impression. During the severe winter of 1947 his mother caught bronchial asthma which never left her; that year, the Kinnocks moved to a new prefabricated Tredegar council bungalow nearer to the town centre which at that time seemed ostentatious because it had a bath, central heating, and a smokeless grate; people used to walk miles just to look at the estate. The building was, however, only meant to be temporary, and Kinnock later noted with disgust that it was still standing many years after it was supposed to have been demolished.

Academically, Kinnock did not shine at junior school, but in 1953 he was considered sufficiently clever to sit the eleven-plus examination. He passed and gained a place at Tredegar Grammar School, but as he was among the top thirty of the hundred eleven-plus exam successes in Mid-Glamorganshire his parents were invited to send him to take the special entrance examination, which he passed, for the prestigious Lewis Boys' Grammar School in Pengam. Lewis School was the best grammar school in South Wales, proud of its sporting and academic values and its emphasis on excellence. Kinnock claims that he hated the school and that it gave him an abiding dislike and mistrust of middle-class institutions. Speaking in the House of Commons many years later, he claimed the school magazine was very misleading. It was about as useful as *Pravda*, in that it listed only the successes: there was no such thing as failure. Kinnock has often claimed that he rebelled against the system and was frequently disciplined. His teachers state that this is nonsense: he is remembered as a conformer, as being no more rebellious than average; although strong willed, he was basically well behaved. He had to be. His economics teacher and school rugby coach, Bryn Jones, states that he had no choice: Pengam was a strict disciplinarian school, and if you 'kicked against the system you were dead'.

Kinnock hated the elitist school because it set him apart from his friends in Tredegar. It also meant a daily round trip of twenty-six miles – three hours' travelling. He would leave the house at 8 a.m. and not get back until 5 p.m., or later if he was on detention, which he frequently was. However, his parents were vitally concerned with their son's school career. Education was the traditional means to escape poverty in Wales and his parents were determined that he should succeed. When he was sixteen his parents deliberately gave up their holiday so that sufficient money could be scraped together to send him on a school trip to Germany.

It was when he was in his teens that Neil began to take a great interest in politics. Gordon Kinnock and his family were loyal trade unionists and Labour voters, but were never involved with the Labour Party, not even distributing leaflets or canvassing. Although Gordon first took his son to hear Nye Bevan speak at the Tredegar Working Men's Hall when Neil was eight, the Kinnock family do not appear to have had a great interest in politics except in the sense of being anti-Tory. Neil, however, claims that his mother 'was a very radical socialist with a Christian tradition' who had a significant influence on his political thinking. Mrs Kinnock made a habit at election time to getting a Tory car to take her to and from the polling station. On her return home she would kindly invite the driver in for a cup of tea, and then keep him talking for anything up to an hour on the tactical grounds that while he was drinking her tea he was not taking anyone else to vote. At the age of fourteen Kinnock was inspired by reading Aneurin Bevan's *In Place of Fear*; a year later, in 1957, he joined the local Ebbw Vale Labour Party because, he claims, he believed that he had a 'socialist conviction'. Indeed it is part of the Kinnock legend that he joined the Labour Party by lying about his age, as the minimum was supposed to be sixteen. He then began to attend a discussion group in Tredegar run by the National Council of Labour Colleges where miners, factory workers, and trade unionists met to talk. Kinnock would take part in these discussions and it was here that he took an early interest in trade union legislation and showed his gift for arguing with, and winning the confidence of, people older than himself. However, his faith in such fora also showed a narrow-sighted and romanticized view of the working classes and a naïve tendency to venerate the effectiveness of the cloth-cap socialist ideas of the peasant philosophers. At that time a crusade was being fought by the Labour moderates against the Bevanites and unilateralists. Kinnock's hero, Nye Bevan, had just denounced unilateral nuclear disarmament at the 1957 Brighton Labour Party conference. Kinnock was shattered and for a week was in utter misery. In 1981 Kinnock was to receive hate mail similar to that received by Bevan in 1957 and taunts of 'Judas' when his abstention and that of other Labour MPs at the Brighton Party conference lost Benn the deputy leadership.

At school Kinnock did not shine: he was in the 'B' stream doing the minimum amount of work. He longed to leave school and applied for jobs in the coal-mines, the police and even the army. His parents were livid when they saw the application forms. When he only passed three O-levels, in English, history and geography, failing in all other subjects, he was disappointed, but also relieved, as it seemed the perfect reason for leaving school. His parents were furious at their son's O-level results, and made him re-sit them. At the second attempt he gained nine O-levels.

Kinnock began to enjoy school for the first time when he was in the sixth form, where he studied for A-levels in Economics, History and English. He was now developing into something of a showman: he took part in the school production of *Journey's End* and was a star of the school Literary and Debating Society. He had considerable self-confidence, and soon developed the necessary debating skill of thinking on his feet. Those who were at school with him at the time, among them John Dawes, who captained the successful 1971 British Lions' tour of New Zealand, remember him as a brilliant charismatic debater. While Kinnock hated Pengam, where he felt stifled because it was a traditional middle-class school that concentrated on academic achievement and sport, it could be that his dislike of the school was because he wasn't noticeably special at either. Although he was a hearty and enthusiastic rugby player, he had neither the physique nor the ability to play in the school First xv. The school rugby coach, Bryn Jones, remembers him as a keen member of the Second xv, who was usually prop forward, but whose great virtue was that he was so popular and got on so well with everyone that he could be trusted in any position on the field. He never had the ability to get beyond the second division in any sports team, and even then could win no colours or prizes. However, Kinnock was a great sports fanatic and during the school vacations used to play for the Ebbw Vale youth rugby team. After a match in 1960, when the Hereford team were defeated 21 to 7, he was involved in a bar-room fist fight that left him badly scarred.

Unlike many who later aspire to senior cabinet office, Kinnock was not considered bright enough to take the Oxbridge entrance examinations. Bryn Jones recalls that 'Neil was not one of our high flyers'. He sat his A-levels in the summer of 1961, and while awaiting his results took a student vacation job at his father's Ebbw Vale steelworks, where he worked as a labourer in the converter shop and in the cold mills. He was delighted when he learnt that he had done better in his A-levels than expected, passing in all three subjects, with a B grade in both economics and history and a C grade in English. He had done sufficiently well to be accepted for a place at the university of his first choice, University College, Cardiff.

2 · *Cardiff*

Neil Kinnock went to University College, Cardiff, in October 1961 to follow a three-year course for a BA degree in Industrial Relations and History. Although some might consider Cardiff provincial, it was the most prestigious of the Welsh universities, and to have won a place there put him among the young Welsh intellectual elite.

He had been stifled at Pengam but now, at Cardiff, he realized his remarkable power to be liked by everyone. When he appreciated this ability he began to grow politically ambitious. He was an immediate success at the University Debating Society, which used to meet on Friday evenings in the canteen. It was a packed rough house and there were usually crowds of five hundred. As with meetings of the Parliamentary Labour Party, speakers had to shout to make themselves heard. Most new students who joined the society began by listening in order to learn the art of debating: Kinnock simply started talking. He was soon the main Debating Society personality, and several times represented Cardiff in the *Observer* inter-university debating competition. Fellow students at the time remember that in the Debating Society and in the Students' Union, Kinnock campaigned on a whole range of social issues such as support for the Cuban revolution, the banning of South African oranges from the cafeteria, and organizing protests against the imprisonment of Nelson Mandela, the South African nationalist leader. In Cardiff he knew the leaders of the Anti-Apartheid Movement, such as Abdul Minty, and frequently attended Anti-Apartheid meetings; he was concerned also with unilateral nuclear disarmament and campaigned for CND. As his political ideas crystallized at this time, his three main political interests were the CND, the Anti-Apartheid Movement, and the University

Labour Society; and his main political influence was still Aneurin Bevan.

He never met or spoke to Bevan, who died just as Kinnock started at university, but he attended the private funeral of his hero and his memorial service, and by an amazing coincidence was on his way to a history examination when he looked out of the bus he was in and saw Jennie Lee taking Bevan's ashes to be scattered over Tredegar. As has already been mentioned, Kinnock had as a child heard Bevan speak and had read *In Place of Fear* when he was fourteen; he was to be increasingly influenced by Bevan's ideas as he grew older. For this reason it is important to stop for a moment to consider these ideas and to look at Bevan's own career.

Aneurin Bevan was also a child of Tredegar, born in a small cottage there in November 1897 to a mining family, five of whose thirteen children had died at birth. His father died of pneumoconiosis, the terrible coal-dust disease that silts up the lungs, and his family received no compensation. Although Aneurin was working down the mines at thirteen, by diligent study at night school he was also to gain a scholarship to the Labour College in London. On his return to Wales he was seen as an agitator and was unable to return to mining. Nye Bevan was a brilliant debater with a gift for oratory that often carried him away, and his name was soon familiar at the great South Wales miners' conferences, his popularity growing with success. So many miners eventually claimed to have worked on the seams with Bevan that it was calculated that the coalface must have been at least 4 miles long.

Bevan was made a District, and then a County, Councillor, but realizing that the power for reform was with Parliament, he fought to gain the Ebbw Vale nomination, which he did in 1929 at the age of thirty-two. Once in Parliament he devoted much of his time in making strenuous efforts to obtain adequate medical services and compensation for miners' families. During the war he threatened that if the miners did not get a compensation increase, he would lead them on fortnightly strikes. He also demanded that the public schools should be closed to abolish class privilege. His greatest triumph was as Minister of Health and Housing in the post-war

Attlee government where he was the main architect of the National Health Service.

Bevan had defied his critics who claimed that he was just a Welsh windbag but he was never really at ease as a government minister, so he found an opportunity to resign with the young left-winger, Harold Wilson, in April 1951 over the Treasury's insistence on minor cuts in the Health Service in order to finance defence spending. When he resigned Bevan was given a tremendous reception by his constituents for whom he had become a folk hero.

Although Bevan spoke well in Parliament, it was his oratory at public meetings for which he was legendary; at these gatherings he would lose no opportunity to use his outstanding ability to boast of his working-class mining ancestry and to make vicious and bitter attacks on the Conservative middle classes. His notorious Manchester speech, when he called the Conservative Party 'lower than vermin', was thought to have lost Labour at least forty seats in the 1950 election. Bevan achieved a large cult following on the left of the party, but frequently defied Attlee's leadership, and was accused of trying to form a party within a party.

While Bevan was the hero of the constituency Labour Party, because of his attacks on the middle classes he was hounded as public enemy number one by Fleet Street and was disliked by much of the Parliamentary Labour Party who regarded him as an irresponsible loudmouth and a vote loser. He and his supporters despised those leaders whose socialism was acquired through education rather than moral fervour and working-class solidarity. In his later years, as shadow Foreign Secretary, Bevan shocked his supporters when at the 1957 Brighton conference he said he was against unilateral disarmament. His former followers listened to their chief in stunned silence, and then heckled him mercilessly. Bevan, however, continued to disagree with the leadership on most issues, and in the sense that his ideas were dangerous liabilities that frightened the middle-class electorate, and kept Labour from power, he himself was of doubtful worth to Labour's electoral chances. When he died of cancer in 1960 his place as MP for the Welsh constituency of Ebbw Vale was assumed by his faithful lieutenant, Michael Foot.

Bevan's *In Place of Fear*, published in 1952, giving his reasons for resigning, was to be a Bible for the Bevanites and when the book was reissued in 1978, the publishers asked Neil Kinnock to write a new introduction. For there are many parallels between Bevan's life and Kinnock's; in his speeches Kinnock makes lavish use of the words of Bevan; he likes to ask questions in the House on Bevan's favourite subjects, national health, miners' pensions, industrial injury compensation; he likes to boast of his own working-class ancestry and to deride the middle classes in vituperative fashion; he too defied his party leader and in his black attaché case he carries a well-thumbed copy of *In Place of Fear*. Further similarities will become apparent during the course of this book.

At Cardiff University, Kinnock continued to work for the Labour Party, and in his second year was made secretary of the Socialist Society which brought him into contact with the local MP, James Callaghan, then a rising star. Soon Kinnock knew Callaghan and his family well and would often invite him to give talks to his fellow students.

Another influence in his life at this time was Professor R.H. Tawney, a socialist writer and economic historian who had contributed much to the development of British left-wing political thought in the 1930s, and who had been most concerned to change the social system in Britain through new legislation. Those who remember Kinnock at university claim that his speeches were strewn with quotations from Tawney.

During the vacations Kinnock would lionize at meetings of the Tredegar Young Socialists, for he had become something of a local hero, the working-class lad who had escaped from the drudgery of factory life to the awesome academic world. However, not all his time was spent talking. He did vacation jobs to supplement his grant and at one time worked as a labourer on a school building site, where he took part in a strike for a pay increase. The employers' representative told the assembled workers there would be no more cash. Kinnock remembers the shop steward standing in front of the school, which had great plateglass windows, telling the assembled building workers: 'We do not want any violence in this dispute, so I want you to ignore completely that pile of gravel by you.'

Kinnock did very little academic work at university, where his record of attendance at lectures was poor: instead, he claims, 'I had a hell of a good time'. Rather than study, he took a great deal of interest in student politics, undergraduate practical jokes, folk music, cricket and rugby. He also had many girl friends at this time. He claims he was good at chatting them up, and was able to do 'a fair bit of courting'. Kinnock, who was slightly built and only 5′ 8″, was again not selected to be a member of the First XV rugby team, being better known for his hearty enthusiasm than his ability. He got in with the rugby crowd and did much singing and drinking, hugely enjoying himself and frequently becoming over-excited and emotional. After he had been a few terms at Cardiff he suffered a severe neck injury on the rugby field in the course of an heroic under-the-post incident. As a result he played less, which left more time for politics. There was some concern that he might have damaged his neck further when he had his car accident during the 1983 leadership contest.

At the start of each academic year the Students' Union would arrange a 'freshers' week' of dances and concerts for the new students. There would also be a 'Freshers' Show' of stalls advertising the university societies. In October 1963 Glenys Elizabeth Parry, a former Miss National Savings beauty queen, arrived at Cardiff to begin a degree course in History and Education. She approached Kinnock at the show, asking him 'Are you the man from the Socialist Society?'. He was entranced by the stunningly attractive young brunette whom he found was 'not only lovely to look at, but also delightful to talk to', and determined to pick her up at the Saturday night dance. Unfortunately he had been injured playing rugby that afternoon, and this, combined with the effect of a couple of pints of beer, caused him to swoon and collapse on the dance floor. Glenys, a girl with a sense of humour, offered to walk him back to his digs.

Glenys was born in North Wales, the daughter of Cyril Parry, a railway signalman, who was a union official and secretary of the Anglesey Labour Party. The main influences in her family life were the chapel, the Labour Party, and the trade unions. She had begun campaigning for the CND at the age of sixteen, and had joined the Labour Party a year later. The CND was to be of lasting interest for Glenys, and during the 1983 election she supported CND and visited the Greenham Common peace camp. Neil and Glenys made a formidable team at Cardiff. When he became chairman of the Socialist Society, she was made secretary, thus complementing his public-speaking talents by her administrative skills and shrewd judgment: together they were known as 'the power and the glory'. While canvassing together in the 1964 general election, they were drenched by a bucket of window-cleaning water thrown by a lady screaming her hatred of Jehovah's Witnesses. When a helplessly laughing Glenys said that they were from the Labour Party, she was set upon by the furious lady with a soaking wet washing cloth.

Neil was madly in love with Glenys but the Welsh beauty was more cautious, and one summer vacation there was a lovers' tiff and she went home to her family. He followed her to North Wales in his old Standard Ten where she told him 'You're daft'. However, they continued to see each other.

In his third year at university, although his record of attendance at lectures had improved, Kinnock had growing doubts about his ability to pass his finals. At that time the industrial relations and history BA course was an unclassified degree, for which there were no distinctions or grades, just pass or fail, but it was essential to pass in each paper in order to obtain the degree. Kinnock's fears were justified when he suffered the humiliation of failing the history paper in his final exam. As a result his degree was deferred until he had sat and passed this paper. This did not mean that he failed his degree, as has often been reported, but that he had to resit the exam the following year. As he had already stated that he wanted to do a post-graduate teacher training course, Monmouth Local Education Authority agreed to stretch his grant another year to permit him to have another attempt, which was successful in June 1965. As at the Pengam school, those who taught Kinnock found that he in no sense distinguished himself other than by his ability to talk and be popular with everyone. His Industrial Sociology lecturer, Professor Thomason, remembers that his work was reasonable, and that he was talkative in the seminars, but he was an average student, who showed no sign that he might possibly be a leader of a political party.

As an average student, attending an average university, Kinnock had swept through his degree examinations after four years at the age of twenty-three. This does not compare favourably with other modern British leaders. At Oxford in the 1930s the firebrand young orator, Michael Foot, was considered the most brilliant political figure of his generation. Edward Heath was President of the Oxford Union in 1939, a wartime army Lieutenant-Colonel at the age of twenty-six, then took the highest marks for his year in the Civil Service Extrance Examination. Harold Wilson was the youngest ever Oxford University lecturer at the age of twenty-one, an MP at the age of twenty-nine, then a Cabinet Minister at thirty-one as President of the Board of Trade in the Attlee Government. Margaret Thatcher gained an Oxford science degree, became a research chemist and was called to the Bar before becoming an MP and Minister for Education. Thatcher, Heath and Wilson were meritocrats who had risen from humble, lower-middle-class family origins by sheer hard work and brain power to achieve great office. Kinnock started lower down the ladder and had further to climb; he had, like them, been to grammar school, but he had not made Oxford or an Honours degree: his gift consisted in being a great communicator with the common people.

In 1964, his third year at Cardiff, Kinnock had fought the election for the presidency of the Students' Union as the socialist candidate. But it had been a rushed and ill-prepared campaign and Kinnock had been soundly beaten by Averil Lloyd. This defeat taught him that no election should be taken for granted and that campaigns had to be well organized.

During his extra fourth year, Neil and Glenys gathered together a small caucus of helpers and concentrated on improving welfare conditions at the university. This work and his long humorous speeches at the weekly meetings of the Debating Society brought him much student popularity. In 1965 he tried again for the presidency of the Union fighting on the slogan 'A mandate for change', and in a record poll, the highest for many years, in which 4 per cent of the students voted, he won a convincing victory.

Kinnock was now president of the Students' Union whilst taking a full-time teacher training course at Cardiff: it was to be a hectic time for him. He became interested in constitutional and administrative reforms, founded on meritocratic ideas. He stated:

> As President, I introduced a much more democratic constitution ...
> with representatives from particular years and faculties ... and amongst

those was a requirement that, well not constitutionally, but the whole regime was, that anybody who represented the union anywhere, whether it was in sport, or debating or photography competitions, or NUS conference, had to have a track record. Because I put an end to the swanning around ... I stopped all that nonsense.

During the long vacation, he got his Students' Union committee to prepare events for the academic year that was to begin in October 1965. A minor Kinnock reform was the 'freshers' tea party'. In previous years the drill had been that the principal of the University would make a long formal speech, welcoming the new students, and then there would be an official tea party. Kinnock disliked any form of middle-class ceremony, and during his presidential year the unfortunate principal was allocated five minutes in which to give the freshers a sense of pride in the University, before Kinnock with a thanks and a farewell dismissed him and his colleagues from the stage. Kinnock then welcomed the freshers and introduced his committee. In the evening, a singing party had been arranged for the blushing new students. The folk group did not appear, so he led the singing of the bawdy songs with unprintable lyrics. He justifiably took the credit for a successful 'freshers' week' that culminated in a University dance featuring the pop group Brian Poole and the Tremeloes. Kinnock also instituted various other minor reforms such as having the union offices redecorated and making improvements in the cafeteria and bar, which at that time was selling Rhymney Bitter at 1s. 7d. a pint. During his term as president he magnanimously permitted his office to be demolished so that the students' bar could be enlarged. The general impression was that his reforms were practical and broadly welcomed.

Kinnock continued his activities as a student protester in November 1965, leading a demonstration of chanting students with placards through the streets of Cardiff against Ian Smith's Rhodesian policy. That month, in his presidential capacity he attended the National Union of Students' conference at Margate and spoke against the Wilson government's plans to introduce a system of loans for students in higher education. Unlike many ambitious student politicians, Kinnock did not seek to advance his career by trying for office on the NUS; instead, he concentrated his attentions on the Labour Party. Glenys was now chairwoman of the NUS in Cardiff, where she was widely praised as a competent and innovative administrator, introducing the idea of a Sixth Form Conference, which was the first of its kind in Wales. This scheme, which she organized in great detail, was considered a triumph, and took the form of seventy school delegates attending a conference at the university to hear talks from careers masters. Neil also took part and his humorous speeches attracted a good deal of awe from the sixth formers. Another of his administrative duties was to welcome a visiting party of Russian students to Cardiff. Kinnock, who most certainly had never been a communist, apparently favoured the enterprise because he claimed it showed 'admiration for the Russian students' courage and determination in saving for five years' to make the visit.

However competent he was in the administration of the Union, he was to find that its actual government was to cause him such difficulties that he was eventually forced to resign. During the 1970s and later, when making his bid for the Labour leadership, it became part of the Kinnock legend that people would travel far and wide to hear his public speech-making. But he had the greatest difficulty in getting the intelligent students at Cardiff to bother to come to his meetings. The routine administration of the Students' Union was carried on by him and his executive committee but the Union's constitution stated that executive actions had to be ratified by a minimum quorum of Student Union members.

Despite the constant advertising of Union general meetings and Kinnock's renown as a speaker, from the beginning of the academic year in October 1965 it became impossible to get a sufficient number of students to Union meetings for crucial decisions to be made or changes to be finalized. Kinnock found his term of office plagued by apathy, the common complaint of student politics. Worse still, when a quorum was convened, members squabbled interminably amongst themselves over constitutional procedures. Then as soon as closing time at the bar drew near, the students drifted away, the essential quorum dissolving before much of the agenda had been discussed.

Kinnock felt that it was 'a disgusting state of affairs when people over the age of 18 can't conduct their own affairs'. The lack of attendance and constant squabbling caused him to adopt desperate measures. In December he threatened to close the Union and put an embargo on its activities until a quorate meeting could be held. This apparently seems to have worked as by February he had improved the methods of getting students to his meetings to pass new legislation. This took the form of ordering the bar to be closed for the evening and threatening to have all the lights in the building switched off at the mains, except those in the canteen where the Union was meeting. These dictatorial measures brought him a certain amount of unpopularity.

Matters were not improved when a section of the Union bar floor collapsed because of dry rot, and building work that he had authorized was still being done at the beginning of the spring term. The slightest incident would be used to embarrass him. On another occasion he was criticized for his lapses in attention to detail when it was found that a senior member of the Union committee was not even a student at the university. As a result of the style of his administration, a small but vocal left-wing anti-Kinnock clique developed, and he was personally attacked in the editorial of the Cardiff student newspaper, which wrote at the time 'Mr Kinnock – I'm sorry – you're going to have to go. It's no good. ... Resign, Kinnock.' It then began to publish a series of allegorical and abusive articles concerning his rise to power in union politics.

That autumn Margot Esher, a twenty-four-year-old post-grad-uate student from Bradford, started a course at the University. The student newspaper reported that she was politically much further to the left than Kinnock, and had ambitions to get on to the executive of the National Union of Students. She rapidly became a major force in the politics of the Cardiff Students' Union, and gained the chairmanship of a charity called World University Service, the entire committee of which resigned shortly afterwards. The anti-Kinnock faction increased during early 1966, constantly wrangling over procedures at Union committees, and frequently personally attacking the president. Kinnock appeared to lack the intellectual stamina and mental agility to do battle over nitty-gritty constitutional issues, preferring the broad sweep of his own speech-making; for several weeks he contemplated giving in his notice as president. The opportunity for resignation occurred suddenly in March. Glenys, as chairman of the local Cardiff branch of the NUS, had, with her committee, recommended a list of delegates to go to the NUS Easter conference. This delegation did not include Margot Esher, who would thus not be entitled to stand for election to the NUS executive. When the Cardiff Union council passed a resolution (which was much later found to be unconstitutional) agreeing that she should have voting rights on the delegation, Kinnock resigned. Of this episode he states,

> Glenys, as NUS chairman, recommended a list of delegates who had a proven record of service, manning welfare bureaux, travel bureaux, and so on, giving up lunchtimes, leisure time, being student councillors, all [of] whom had earned their place on the delegation. The proposition was that others who had not had a proven record, in Cardiff, of such service [should go too], and Glenys advised the Students' Representative Council that in the event of the people of proven worth not going then she would resign. So it wasn't a question of who else was to go, it was a question of who deserved to go. And she said that she would resign if these people weren't going ... and it was perfectly her constitutional right to submit the list ... I had given the Student Representative Council, in my constitutional changes, the power to ratify the lists.

Kinnock formally resigned as president. Glenys also handed in her notice, taking the whole of her committee with her. The consequence of his resignation was that his left-wing rival, Margot Esher, was able to stand for election at the NUS conference. While Kinnock had resigned as a matter of principle to protect Glenys, it is arguable that it would have shown more political determination to have remained as president and fought. However, the effort of leading an unwilling army was too much of a strain and he threw in the towel. The reasons he gave at the time for resigning were the matter of principle over the NUS, and the generally bored attitude and lack of interest of the students and council. The opinion of the Cardiff students in general was that Kinnock had been a good president, and that he and Glenys had done much for the Union during their time in office. Kinnock had already decided that there was little worthwhile political advance to be had in student politics; his next priority was to concentrate on the Labour Party, and to find himself a job.

Teaching suited Kinnock's personality, and in the tradition of many Welsh politicians he hoped it would assist his political ambitions. In the spring of 1966 he gained his Teaching Certificate, achieving an A grade for teaching practice, and a C grade for education. He went for several interviews; he was offered a job as a teacher at a school in Ebbw Vale, and also one at a college of Further Education at Cirencester, which he seriously considered accepting, but he turned both these down in favour of a job with the Workers' Educational Association in South Wales. The senior officials of the WEA in this district were also senior in the local Labour Party, and though Kinnock had to do the full procedure of job interviews, and was awarded his appointment entirely on merit, he was immediately seen by these officials as a personality who would have a future with the Labour Party.

The Workers' Educational Association was founded as a charity in 1903 in order to augment the education of the working man through local non-political evening discussion groups. There were no academic requirements and no examinations: classes of no more than forty members would commit themselves to 'sustained study at a high academic level over a period of three years'. Its president for many years, and the Labour Party's educational adviser, was Kinnock's philosopher hero, Tawney, who said of the WEA: 'The friendly smittings [discussions] of weavers, potters, miners and engineers have taught me much about the problems of political and economic science which cannot easily be learned from books.' The golden years of the WEA were the 1930s, when there were branches in most British towns. Fourteen members of the post-war Labour Government and seventy Labour MPs had at one time been with the WEA as tutors or students. Since then, the need for such a form of education had become something of an historical anachronism, although even when Kinnock was a teacher there were still several MPs in the House of Commons who had once been involved with the WEA.

In August 1966 Kinnock began his job as a WEA tutor-organizer. The job exactly suited his qualifications, his interest in adult education, and his degree in Industrial Relations and History. He dashed about South Wales in his green minivan, tutoring classes in Carmarthenshire on 'Britain and the World Economy'; in Merthyr on 'The Psychology of Industry'; in Abergavenny on 'Trade Unions and the Law' and in Glamorganshire on 'The British Economy'. Kinnock was enthusiastic about his job although he might have to spend thirty hours a week organizing and preparing classes and forty hours a week teaching. Many of his pupils were middle-aged trade unionists who were quick to argue with the young graduate, but he was greatly liked; he described his work as probably the most enjoyable job that he could have chosen.

Neil and Glenys were married on 25 March 1967 at Holyhead, Anglesey. It was agreed that there should be a quiet chapel wedding, as neither wanted an elaborate service. The guest of honour was the local Labour MP, Cledwyn Hughes. Glenys had by now completed her Diploma in Education at Cardiff and was teaching at Abersychan Grammar School, so the newly-weds decided to get a small house at Pontllanfraith, some ten miles south of Tredegar, which would be convenient for Glenys's school and central for Neil's travels to his various classes. Their work for the Labour Party continued and both were invited to stand for the local Mynyddislwyn Urban District Council, which was in the area of Pontllanfraith, where they lived. The trouble for Neil was the amount of evening work he had to do for the WEA. Glenys, too, was in the early years of teaching and was doing a great deal of class preparation. So both of them turned down the offers.

Kinnock had helped to establish a WEA class in economics at Pontllanfraith. Here he met some of his closest political friends in the Labour Party. The class also proved his most successful, as three of his students, among them Barry Moore, who was later to become his election agent, went on to Coleg Harlech and later got degrees. The Young Turks of the small Pontllanfraith group were Bevanites, but, like the 'revisionists' of the 1950s, they saw the importance of gradual development in the Labour Party. They campaigned against a number of government policies, such as pit closures, and believed that the Wilson government was wasting its time in office by not implementing socialist policies. At the local Bedwellty Labour Party meetings, the Young Turks attempted to get practical administrative reforms introduced. There appeared to be some necessity for this as the local MP, Harold Finch, had faced action in the High Court because of overspending in the 1964 general election. At this time Kinnock used to help Michael Foot, who with his wife, television producer Jill Craigie, had moved to Tredegar in 1960 when the veteran left-winger became MP for Ebbw Vale (Kinnock had first met Foot in 1963). Neil and Glenys would go on walks with Michael and Jill Foot, and friends who knew them at the time claim that the Foots saw Kinnock almost as the son they had never had.

As a party member and junior official in his local party, Kinnock was a popular and hardworking constituency member who did much public speaking to help the Labour Party in South Wales, which was being increasingly threatened by the Welsh nationalist party Plaid Cymru. In July 1968 a by-election occurred at Caerphilly, and there were fears that Plaid Cymru might win despite Labour's previous 21,148 majority. The Caerphilly party asked for Kinnock's help, as he was known as a formidable public speaker who could deal with hecklers.

During the bitterly fought election Kinnock won the respect and admiration of party workers. There were many who thought that he himself would make an able MP, and would become a future power in the Labour Party, but few at that stage saw him as a cabinet minister. He is remembered for his charm, sense of fun, wit, and enthusiasm. He worked hard at his canvassing, at which he was superb, showed natural powers of leadership, was a great motivator and winner of votes. Labour just held on to Caerphilly with a majority of 1,874, but for Kinnock the election was a personal triumph and it had made his name with the South Wales Labour Party establishment.

At this time, 1968, he made his media debut, first on a BBC farming programme, and then on a local commercial television show 'On the Bridge', which took the form of conversations in a pub, with Kinnock as the most prominent speaker. It was also in 1968 that it occurred to him for the first time that he might stand for Parliament. Whilst he was tutoring a WEA class in a neighbouring constituency, some of the class, who were trade union shop stewards and older Labour Party workers, suggested that he should stand for selection as a candidate.

A surprise opportunity arose in February 1969 when, at a Bedwellty constituency meeting where Kinnock happened to be taking the minutes, the popular and much loved member, Harold Finch, said during 'any other business' that he intended to retire before the next election as he had reached the age of seventy. Bedwellty constituency consisted of fifteen self-sufficient towns and villages based on the coal and steel industries. However, these were what Hunter Davies had described as 'left-overs from the glacier of the industrial revolution' and were now suffering from a series of pit closures. Bedwellty was among the safest Labour seats in the country; in the 1966 general election Finch had won with a massive 25,000 majority. The Young Turks immediately went to the Llan-arth Road Club to decide what to do. It was agreed that Kinnock should make a bid for the nomination. However, the favourite to win the constituency was miners' agent Lance Rogers, aged forty-three, who had got the official nomination of the National Union of Mineworkers. This was critical as local MPs had, as a matter of habit, been NUM nominations; Finch and his predecessor, Sir Charles Edwards, had been miner candidates and traditions died hard in South Wales.

Kinnock's age was against him, but he was able to win the nomination of the Transport and General Workers' Union, which he had joined a few months earlier. He had much support among the younger members of the constituency party, and among his WEA pupils who canvassed the trade unions. He also made arrange-ments to invite the Minister for the Arts, Jennie Lee, Aneurin Bevan's widow, to speak at a special meeting, in early March, at Cardiff University on the subject of education. The constituency party drew up a list of nine candidates. But it was soon clear that the contest was going to be a bitter fight between Lance Rogers and Kinnock, whose supporters knew it would be a struggle against the odds. What has not been generally known is that in the first ballot there were four candidates, Kinnock and Rogers, Keith Griffiths, a Coal Board clerk, and Dengar Evans, a pharmaceutical chemist. During the ballot on 11 June Kinnock received by far the highest number of votes, but not the decisive majority that he needed to win. Griffiths and Evans were eliminated, but though Rogers and Kinnock were invited to speak, this seems to have been regarded as a mere formality because it was thought that Griffiths's and Evans's votes would pass to Rogers, and Kinnock would be defeated. However, the Kinnock public speaking magic worked, for in the second ballot the result was a draw with 75 votes to Rogers and 75 to Kinnock. Dozens of people had switched their vote to Kinnock, although his agent, Barry Moore, later stated with some bitterness that the number of people who eventually claimed to have voted for Kinnock was greater than the total number of votes cast. Kinnock's supporters asked Glenys whether they should demand a postponement in the hope of getting more votes, but she told them to press on. The candidates were again invited to speak for ten minutes. Rogers went over the same speech again. Kinnock, however, in probably the most crucial speech of his career, made a brilliant imaginative flight of oratory. When the final ballot was cast, the votes were Rogers 74, Kinnock 76. At the age of twenty-seven Kinnock had won the nomination for one of the safest seats in Britain. It meant that he could, if he wished, be a Member of Parliament for the rest of his working life. The first thing Neil and Glenys did when the result was announced was to go to the telephone booth across the road from the selection meeting and ring Kinnock's parents. Mary Kinnock was delighted and said Neil should take Glenys home as she was then several months pregnant and give her a cup of tea. Neil then spoke to his father and said 'Westminster next stop, Dad'. The answer was, 'Oh, you never know, people can be funny. Now take Glenys home and get her feet up.' Kinnock admires this attitude of his father, whose reaction to everything was one of caution.

The struggle for the nomination had caused a great deal of bitterness in the constituency, but once Kinnock had been nominated, the party workers pulled together. It was not until after his nomination that many miners realized that he was by far the best candidate. Although his election to Parliament was now a formality, he energetically threw himself into campaigning, as he was naturally energetic, he wanted to prove himself, and he believed it was the duty of MPs and prospective parliamentary candidates to campaign hard for the Labour Party. His effectiveness as a Labour speaker was such that although he himself had not yet been elected to Parliament, he was already being invited to speak in other Welsh constituencies to support their local MPs. His self-confidence, courage, popularity and ability were such that he could even win a standing ovation from audiences whose views were opposed to his own. At one such meeting of the Caerphilly Plaid Cymru branch in March 1970 he called for 'Welshmen of radical opinion and democratic intent' to unite in opposition to Conservatism. He said 'The Tory winner-take-all philosophy' would have disastrous implications for the Welsh economy: 'Even the most devout nationalist must prefer government by the Parliament at Westminster to government by the City of Westminster.'

Having won the nomination, Kinnock made his first speech as prospective parliamentary candidate to his constituency party at Pontllanfraith. While generally seen as a left-winger, he immediately showed signs of pragmatism, even towards the trade unions of whom he was a lifelong supporter. He spoke to a meeting of shop stewards of the Foundry Workers' Union at Blackwood in September 1969, warning them that the popular image of the shop steward as a 'pig-headed machine' had to be erased because it was dangerous since it made the public demand for restrictions on trade union actions credible and respectable. 'British trade unionism,' he declared, 'is facing one of the most critical periods in its history.' He said that a strong trade union movement was fundamental to modern British democracy because it was one of the few continuous methods of representation available to the working classes. He argued that if the image of trade unionism had been tarnished by union leaders and shop stewards, it was in the power of ordinary members to alter that image, and if they wished to retain their working rights they had better get on with that job. As a prospective parliamentary candidate with an election approaching, Kinnock's oratory was turned on the Conservatives. In February 1970 he launched a strong attack, at a constituency meeting, on the Conservatives' pre-election promises of tax and price cuts. 'They propose to cut taxes and simultaneously re-establish defence forces east of Suez: this is magic not mathematics.' Kinnock also at this time had formulated, and spoke of, his ideas on defence and foreign policy. There is no historical evidence of this but he has stated since that his views even then were that 'We require a definition of role for Britain, as a medium-sized power, with potentially great world influence, that is commercial and cultural.'

Kinnock had a tendency to be mesmerized by his own speech-making, and much of his campaign rhetoric (or at least that which was reported in the newspapers) at the time bordered on the absurd. Speaking on the subject of race relations to a conference of the Monmouthshire Labour Women's Federation at Cwm, in March 1970, he told delegates that a recently published Registrar-General's report on immigrant births would be 'transcribed into a hymn of race hate' by Enoch Powell. Recently announced Conservative policies for 'abolishing housing subsidies, chopping regional economic aid and encouraging private pension and medical schemes', Kinnock said, all bore the stamp of Enoch Powell. Continuing his attack on the Conservatives, he was ironically to use a phrase that Michael Heseltine used later to describe Kinnock's 'guts at Goose Green' speech. At a public meeting in February 1969 Kinnock described the Conservative decision to use law and order as an election issue as callous 'gutter politics'. To propose law and order as a means of curing national ills was 'at best irrelevant, at worst totalitarian', he said. 'There is more crime prevention in a decent home, good school, a well-equipped neighbourhood and a humane police force than in a whole library of public order acts or a regiment of hangmen.'

The Wilson government's electoral chances in 1969 looked bleak. It was trailing the Conservatives in the opinion polls and loosing a string of by-elections with swings of more than 15 per cent. But even at this late hour, its luck could change, as that of the Conservatives had in the late 1950s when they had recovered from the disaster of Suez to increase their majority from 58 to 100, in the October 1959 election. Early in 1970 Labour fortunes did indeed appear to be on the mend. At the South Ayrshire by-election in March the Conservative swing was only 2.9%. By April opinion polls were showing Labour ahead of the Conservatives for the first time in three years. At the spring local elections Labour for the first time since 1964 was winning seats from the Conservatives. Wilson decided to take a chance and with the agreement of the cabinet and the Parliamentary Labour Party he announced that a general election would be held on 18 June.

Kinnock said the Conservative manifesto, 'A Better Tomorrow', should have been called 'A Bitter Tomorrow', whose promises were incredible and were just 'crocodile tears, half-truths and fairy-tales'. He fought an enthusiastic campaign and produced his own election leaflet with the slogan 'Only Labour is Willing and Able', which had messages from Glenys and Finch, who wrote, hinting darkly of Kinnock's rebellious past, 'I am sure that Neil Kinnock will follow Labour Party policy'. The Mineworkers' Union also issued a leaflet urging their members to vote for Kinnock as the Labour candidate. In the general election of June 1970 the votes cast at Bedwellty were,

N.G. Kinnock (Labour)	28,078
P. Marland (Conservative)	5,799
C. M. Davet (Plaid Cymru)	3,780

For Kinnock the result was a great triumph. Despite the national swing against Labour, he had a 22,279 majority, only some 2,000 votes fewer than the majority of 24,984 that the old campaigner Finch had won in the Labour landslide victory of 1966. Kinnock had done even better than the majority of 20,950 won at Huyton by Labour's unfortunate leader, Harold Wilson. The Labour Party, however, had crashed to defeat. While in 1966 the Wilson government had secured a majority of 95, now the Conservatives were returned to power with a majority of 35. Kinnock resigned from the Workers' Educational Association, where he had continued to work as a teacher until the 1970 general election, and prepared to begin his career at Westminster.

3 · Parliament

Kinnock, at just twenty-eight, was one of the Labour Party's youngest Members of Parliament. He had never been to the House of Commons until elected, and found the procedure there so totally confusing that it took him months to comprehend it. He has stated,

> I had always had, at the back of my mind, Nye Bevan's description that upon arriving, the young Member of Parliament is reminded of being in church. And ... of course Parliament is a church, dedicated to the most reactionary of all religions, ancestry worship. And I didn't arrive with any particular instinct for irreverence, although Bevan advised that you should cultivate irreverence. But my initial impression was of buzzing confusion, of inadequate working circumstances, and very little else because I just got on with the task of being a constituency Member of Parliament.

Trembling with nervousness, he rose in the House of Commons on 13 July 1970 to make his maiden speech. He said he was pleased to make a speech on the subject of 'health and social security because the House will know that Socialists in my part of the country, South Wales, have made a unique contribution to the design and development of our National Health Service. Though I cannot hope to rival the talents and visions of Jim Griffiths or Aneurin Bevan, I can bring to this House some zeal for social justice and provide a continuity of interest in this subject.'

The Health Service had been the subject of Bevan's first speech to the House of Commons in 1929; it was also to be the main theme of Kinnock's leadership victory speech in October 1983. It was a convention of the House that a maiden speech be made on a non-controversial subject. Kinnock, however, did not waste the opportunity to make a blistering attack on the Conservative Party. He said the Conservatives, who were economically and socially 'pre-

pared to stampede back to the barren prairie lands of *laissez-faire*'
were a 'party whose very existence is an illustration of rapacity and
selfishness'.

Almost immediately on being elected to Parliament, Kinnock
wondered if he had not made a mistake. He acknowledged that he
was too young to be an MP. The sense of purpose seemed to be in
his constituency work, but no matter how much he did to help
people, he seemed to be able to achieve very little. He did not
consider resigning as has sometimes been reported but, he states,
'I acknowledged the fact that there were periods in the whole
Parliament in which I wondered whether I wanted to be doing this
for the rest of my life. Or whether there was a better [contribution]
that I could make. I didn't consider resigning.'

He had to live a miserable life in digs during the week, while
Glenys was at home in Pontllanfraith, bringing up the young
family. The Kinnocks' first child, Stephen, had been born in
January 1970, and their daughter Rachel two years later. Kinnock,
a loyal husband and a devoted father, hated being away from home
and spent as much time with his family as he possibly could. In
October 1971 he did not go to the Labour Party conference, but
instead watched it on television at home. He loathed sleeping under
a different roof from his wife and children. Glenys found things
'miserable and lonely', and Kinnock's work at Parliament was
clearly wrecking family life. He would arrive for the week-end from
London on the 5 a.m. milk train and would have to leave again on
the last bus. Friends acknowledged that he was just trying to do
too much. The Kinnocks also found themselves in financial difficulties, with the cost of the general election campaign, having digs
in London, and keeping a house in Pontllanfraith. Neil could not
even afford to take his family on holiday other than to visit his
mother-in-law at Holyhead.

Meanwhile his mother had retired as a district nurse and with her
husband had moved from the old prefabricated house to Bryn Bach
Street, Tredegar. Then, in 1971, tragedy struck: Gordon Kinnock,
then aged sixty-four, died while still at work; Mary Kinnock died
a week later. Neil was grief-stricken, and the Kinnocks then decided
to leave Bedwellty and move to London. The move created a
sensation in the constituency which the locals still talk about many

years later. Unjustified, cynical, and bitter remarks were made aloud that Kinnock, for all his championing of working-class causes, thought the locals were no longer good enough for him. It was remembered that Finch, until the age of seventy, had attended Parliament during the week and still been able to live in the constituency. It was remembered also that Nye Bevan, in 1954, to hoots of derision from the Conservative press, had quit his native Tredegar and bought a country house in Buckinghamshire. The move caused Kinnock some personal anguish, but he had to put his family first and when he made this clear to his constituents it was gradually accepted. The family moved to a dull suburban semi-detached house at 73 Dysart Avenue, Kingston-upon-Thames. This was made possible by a general salary increase that was awarded to MPs at this time. A small terraced house in Pontllan-fraith was decorated in the Habitat style and maintained as a base for Kinnock's frequent visits to the constituency.

His first four years in Parliament, during the lifetime of the Heath government, were remarkably unspectacular. He worked hard as an MP and as he slowly gathered confidence as a speaker, he rose to his feet in the House more often. He asked written questions on a staggering 239 occasions. He wisely confined his interests to what he knew about and to the welfare of his constituents. He spoke on a wide range of subjects concerning South Wales, such as bus services, road safety, house improvement grants, invalid carriages, and began a campaign, that was to last many years, to get a district general hospital built in Monmouthshire. His questions tended to follow the tradition of Nye Bevan in trying to get a better deal for Coal Board widowed pensioners. He continued his interest in education and asked questions concerning nursery schools, handicapped children, and free school milk, of the then unnoticed Secretary of State for Education, Margaret Thatcher. Continuously during 1971 he urged that an atmospheric pollution survey be established for South Wales. There had been medical reports of unaccountable illnesses among people in the locality, and Kinnock hoped that a Glamorgan survey could establish whether there were links between heavy metals, such as lead, mercury, and cadmium in the atmosphere and the general level of health in the area. His most constant interest during this time he considers to have been for Welsh regional development policy – 'I think I strung together some fair speeches about industrial development', he states. He was concerned to see better co-ordination between the Department of Trade and Industry and the Welsh and Scottish Offices on regional development matters. An early success was an intelligent and well-argued letter on the subject of Welsh regional development that was published in *The Times* within a week of his being elected to Parliament.

While Kinnock worked long hours at Parliament and was diligent in the care of his constituents over a wide range of issues, a small number of slightly comical events brought him to the notice of the general public and landed him with the image of being something of an irresponsible clown.

His first mention by a national newspaper was in a brief article which appeared in the *Guardian* in March 1971. It reported that Kinnock, who had a 'fine Welsh sense of catastrophe', was starting a one-man campaign to improve the first-aid facilities for the people who worked at the Palace of Westminster. He wanted a proper medical centre established, and claimed that he would be creating hell were Parliament a factory in his constituency, employing several hundred people with no full-time nurse. He took a certain amount of pleasure in humiliating priggish ministers, and took a leading part in a debate on the subject of the House of Commons canteen, concerning the price of ham sandwiches.

While Kinnock had no need to worry about the constituency since he had won by such a substantial majority, he was almost fanatical in his concern for his constituents. A few weeks after being elected as an MP he cancelled his first parliamentary trip overseas to the Sudan because of heavy commitments in his constituency. He would have 'surgeries' for those who wanted to see him every other week-end, and the venues and dates of surgery meetings, for months ahead, would be posted prominently about the constituency. The most frequent difficulties were to do with housing state benefits, health, telephones, and concessionary coal. He would listen with sincere concern and would sometimes there and then write a letter on House of Commons notepaper to the relevant authority.

At university Kinnock had invented a more democratic and

accountable Union constitution; he had also, for many years, believed in having wider democracy for the constituency Labour parties. In Finch's time the Bedwellty general management committee would meet just once a year, when it would elect a committee that would operate the constituency. Kinnock, who believed in politics by stealth, like the 'Revisionists' of the 1950s, introduced a system of GMC meetings twice a year at first, then quarterly. By the time the local party realized what was happening, the GMC was meeting almost every month. Kinnock believed that an MP should be accountable but not subservient to the wishes of his local constituency party, and he would give a regular 'parliamentary report' at each GMC of what he had been doing at the Commons. This local accountability did not just apply to the local Labour Party. Each September he would arrange public meetings at three or four places in the constituency, at which he would speak on his work as an MP.

Kinnock's dissatisfaction and feeling of helplessness in Parliament continued until the miners' strike gave his time at Westminster a sense of purpose. As he says, 'The time when I really felt it worth me being there was after the miners' work-to-rule started in 1971, and I became directly and closely involved with the course of the miners' dispute, and that's when it really occurred to me that there was some point.'

With his knowledge of trade union matters and as MP for a coal-mining constituency, he was asked by the Miners' Union to put their case, which he did at public meetings throughout Britain, although his own union was the TGWU. Speaking in a House of Commons debate on the Emergency Powers Act, he claimed it was not the miners who were holding the country to ransom but the Government. South Wales miners' leader Emlyn Williams recalls that Kinnock accepted every invitation to speak at meetings, he 'spoke on every platform,' and did everything he could to help the miners.

In 1970 he helped Michael Foot, who had spent twenty-five years as a backbench MP, make a successful attempt at election to the shadow cabinet. Kinnock initially aligned himself with the left of the Parliamentary Party and was an enthusiastic attender of Tribune Group meetings, even writing an article on the group for its newspaper *Tribune*.

The Tribunites, whom he described as the 'light cavalry of the Parliamentary Party', had grown considerably since the Labour Government had been defeated in 1970. An informal group of some eighty democratic socialist MPs from the left of the party came together every week at the House of Commons. Meetings were informal and noisy, contributions were short, and voices were counted to provide a consensus. There was no discipline because members would tolerate none.

An early success of Kinnock's was the publication in the autumn of 1971 of an obscure pamphlet, 'Wales and the Common Market', which he wrote with several other Welsh MPs. The pamphlet argued that membership of the Common Market would not be in Wales's interest. Kinnock's view was that economically membership of the EEC was a gamble that Wales could not afford to take. Unlike many of the Labour left, Kinnock was not distrustful of Europeans, but believed that there was no certainty that the chances of prosperity would be improved, nor was there a guarantee that political autonomy would be retained, so he was strongly opposed to EEC entry. His attitude was cautious; his main criticism of the EEC was that the forecasts for it were irresponsibly optimistic. In what was almost a left-wing Conservative attitude, he expressed dissatisfaction with the Government's belief that the short-term costs would be high and the long-term benefits great. He was not clear on what time-scale these beliefs were based nor whether any distant benefits were guaranteed. For those searching for evidence of Kinnock the pragmatist, rather than Kinnock the dyed-in-the-wool left-winger, this is an important find. It showed that he put the Welsh national interest before that of party policy.

His argument was that Wales had always been a victim of 'market effects' and it could not afford the gamble. For Wales, a United Kingdom economic boom did not historically mean automatic growth, but a national slump always meant contraction. There was good reason for concern, especially as post-war development had not happened because of private commercial initiatives but because of public regional decisions made in Parliament.

What Kinnock's opposition to the Common Market did show was a pragmatic recognition of the erosion of Wales's economic base and the grim necessity of its dependence on government assistance. Although his cautious view was essentially orientated towards Wales, his view could also be applied to Britain, and this assessment was fundamentally correct. His belief was that reform of the Common Agricultural Policy should be the minimum acceptable incentive for Britain to remain in the Common Market. During the 1983 leadership campaign he was to drop his opposition to Britain's EEC membership, believing that withdrawal was no longer feasible. But up until then he had been among the most energetic of Labour MPs in criticizing Labour pro-marketeers. In June 1972, then aged thirty and still one of the youngest Labour MPs, he angrily stated at a weekly Parliamentary Labour Party meeting that he had 'suspicions' that there had been secret negotiations between Labour pro-marketeers and the Government to see that the Common Market Bill would not be defeated. Despite immediate denials by leading pro-marketeers, he criticized the MPs further at a public meeting in Ebbw Vale. He stated that the pro-market MPs who failed to support Labour in divisions on the Bill were 'quislings'. These 'dirty dozen', as he dubbed them, had permitted the Tories to win vital votes and kept the Heath government in power. Kinnock said: 'It is stretching credibility too far to imagine that any of this could have been accomplished without the willingness of one or more Labour MPs to enter into a conspiracy.' Such MPs, he asserted, showed a calculated contempt for the Labour movement.

However, although several constituency Labour parties had promised retribution against the ninety Labour pro-marketeers, Kinnock did not believe that the party conference should reprimand the MPs or that they should be hounded from the Party. To him an MP's right to act according to his conscience was paramount. He believed that while MPs should consult their local parties as much as possible, this did not mean that an MP should merely be a delegate of his constituency party. This was a belief that he had maintained from the start of his parliamentary career. He stated this in a letter to *The Times* in September 1972. In terms of the argument which was to take place at the time of the 1981 deputy leadership, it is difficult to understand why the far left should have been surprised that Kinnock defied his constituency party. His letter to *The Times* reads:

The Conference will reaffirm the Party's long-held attitude that MPs are not delegates. At the same time it will tell MPs in the direct language of rank-and-file activists: 'We collect, canvass and campaign. Some of us jeopardize domestic life and promotion prospects. We selected you and got enough voters to the polls to elect you. We do not wish to shackle you, we frequently agree with your dissension and we usually defend your independent action because we respect your convictions. But do not think of us as a mere 'Party label round your neck', noted and then ignored. We accept your right to dissent, but you must acknowledge our right to hold you accountable. Do not take us for granted.

In the winter of 1973 the Conservative government were again in conflict with the National Union of Mineworkers, concerning a wage demand of £45 per week. At a major parliamentary debate in November 1973, Kinnock found himself the only MP representing a coal-mining constituency, and was able to give a detailed set of facts and figures of conditions in the coal industry. He described Edward Heath as being 'in his Führer-bunker of arrogance behind his last-ditch defences of the Industrial Relations Act, the Counter Inflation Act and the Emergency Powers Act'. He continued his bitter attacks against the Prime Minister, whom he accused of opposing the miners for a 'short-term aim by trying to bring public criticism down upon the heads of miners and other industrial workers in strife, who are good servants of this country'. The government decided to settle the matter by a general election in 1974.

Kinnock was now just beginning to make a minor name for himself in the party; he appeared in a televised Labour Party political broadcast and toured his constituency with a loudspeaker car blaring the pop song 'Part of the Union'. At the February 1974 general election the votes cast in his constituency were:

N.G. Kinnock (Labour)	26,664
T.S. Yeo (Conservative)	5,027
R. Morgan (Liberal)	5,020

Kinnock had won by a majority of 21,637 in an election that saw the Conservative government swept from office.

4 · Devolution

Labour had won the February 1974 election by 5 seats but the result obscured the long-term decline of the Labour Party. Since the time of Attlee, Labour's percentage of the vote in General Elections had been declining. In February 1974 it had attracted only 37% of the vote, which was lower than in any election since 1931. Although Wilson fought another general election in the autumn of 1974, Labour scarcely did any better, remaining in power with a miniscule majority. Labour's ability to win general elections at this time was helped by the Conservatives who had not had a nationally popular leader since the time of Macmillan. Although of doubtful success as a Prime Minister, Wilson's great achievement during the years 1963–75 as Labour leader was as a party manager, holding the Party together during a period of great change and instability in British politics and steering it through to win three out of four elections. A cunning intellectual, Wilson achieved this by carefully balanced creative tension, nullifying left-wingers by bringing them into the Government and binding them to collective responsibility and ministerial jobs in which they could not compromise politically. However successful in maintaining an administration, Wilson's reputation for manipulation of his colleagues bred the disloyalty and mistrust of much of the Labour Party. Labour MPs of the Tribune left were especially critical of the policies of the Wilson governments. As for Kinnock, though as leader in 1983 he made pleas for party unity, he had earlier in his parliamentary career several times led campaigns against his own Labour government.

He had fought a successful election for Labour. He had proved his worth on television party political broadcast programmes, and was acknowledged to have been one of the brightest young MPs of the 1970 parliament. In March 1974 he was given the honour of being asked to second the Labour government's motion of thanks to the Queen's Speech. When the new Labour government was formed he was asked by several ministers if he wished to gain experience by serving as a parliamentary private secretary. However, he disagreed with the Wilson administration on several matters and had little wish to serve in it.

While the ninety or so cabinet and junior ministers, which make up the total government team, are appointed by the Prime Minister, each cabinet minister can if he wishes appoint an MP from the governing party to serve as his PPS. As an unsalaried honorary appointment, being a PPS helps to get an MP's name known and is usually considered to be a useful apprenticeship for an ambitious junior minister. As Kinnock had no wish to serve in the Labour Government even as a PPS, he told ministers who offered him appointments as a PPS that he had already agreed to be the PPS of Employment Secretary Michael Foot. He then spoke to Foot, who said: 'But I don't want a PPS'. Foot however agreed that Kinnock should be his PPS, but with a private understanding that this should only be for a year. Kinnock soon regretted having taken the PPS job, as he wanted to be free to criticize the Wilson-led Parliamentary Labour Party on a number of issues, such as the social contract and notably devolution.

The Labour Government were increasingly worried about the rapid growth of nationalism in Scotland and Wales. Labour's failure to improve employment and welfare conditions after its return to office in 1964 had disillusioned many members of the Scottish working class and also the intellectuals; this growth in support for the nationalists in Scotland had been at the cost of seats for Labour. The Scottish Nationalist Party, which was formed in 1928, had been a very minor party until an SNP candidate won a by-election in Hamilton in 1967. Then in 1970 the SNP received 11.4% of the vote in Scotland and sent one MP to Westminster; this increased to 21.9% in the vote in February 1974, and 7 MPs.

The Kilbrandon Commission on the Constitution, which Wilson had set up in 1968, reported in October 1973, recommending administrative and legislative devolution for Wales and Scotland. Kinnock was opposed to this and said in Parliament that there was 'no large body of opinion, at least in Wales, that wants a half-baked, overgrown county council with no effective powers'. However, support for the nationalists in Scotland continued to increase, and in the October 1974 general election the SNP won 30.4% of the Scottish vote and gained 11 seats. The SNP was second in 42 constituencies, 35 of them held by Labour. Given that British governments could be elected with little more than 30% of the popular vote, the Government were fearful that if the nationalists were not placated with some form of assembly, they could claim majority support for independence, and present the British Government with a *fait accompli* of a UDI. The scale of organized nationalism in Wales was far less, but of sufficient concern to the Labour government to include it in its devolution proposals. In Labour's October 1974 election manifesto Wilson committed the party to creating 'elected assemblies in Scotland and Wales'. Separate manifestos were also published for Scotland and Wales, giving more detailed proposals. It was Labour that had the most to lose in Wales, where it held 27 of the 35 seats. The Welsh Nationalists, Plaid Cymru, had received 11.5% of the Welsh vote in 1970, but unlike the Scottish Nationalists, had failed to make any advances in the 1974 general elections, beyond their hard core of supporters: in February they won 10.8% of the vote in Wales, and in October only 10.7%.

Although Kinnocks's opposition to devolution was well-meaning, he did not seem to understand how crucial the nationalists' votes were for the Labour Government's survival in Parliament. Labour did not have a decisive majority in the House of Commons for the entire five-year parliament from 1974 until the 1979 general election; during this time it depended on the minority parties, the Liberals, Ulster Unionists, and the Scottish and Welsh Nationalists. Anticipating trouble, Wilson had got the entire Welsh Parliamentary Labour Party to sign a paper on devolution before the February 1974 election. But when the new draft White Paper on devolution was published in 1975, Kinnock publicly argued with Wilson, in the House of Commons, that it bore no resemblance to the agreement that had been signed earlier.

Kinnock's disagreement with the Labour policy of devolution for Wales was to be critical for his career. For almost the entire lifetime of the 1974-9 Labour government, until devolution was rejected by public referendum in March 1979, as a junior MP he single-handedly fought an eventually successful campaign against his Government's plans for Welsh devolution. Labour's devolution plans created a dilemma for Kinnock, as it meant having to fight the October 1974 general election on a manifesto containing a policy with which he disagreed. In his election leaflet he said: 'We will meet the genuine demands for new democratic developments with an elected Welsh Assembly.' However, at every public meeting he spoke of his own misgivings on devolution and promised to let the Welsh people decide. He accused Plaid Cymru of only flirting with devolution, when what they really wanted was independence. He said at a public meeting, 'In the last half-century of Ulster we have learned that legislative autonomy without economic solvency and the support of the whole community is a bloody tragedy. Neither precondition is met in Wales and that fact will sink separatism and disciples.' Not only was Kinnock himself opposed to devolution, but so were most of his constituents. In Glamorganshire and Gwent devolution seemed an irrelevance, and there was little sympathy for Plaid Cymru.

Welsh Nationalism was usually synonymous with the speaking of the Welsh language. In North Wales, from where the nationalists drew much of their support, the Welsh language was spoken by most of the local population, although further south less than 10% could speak it. In June 1974 a County rates federation, sick of having official forms in Welsh and too much Welsh on television, wrote to Kinnock asking for a referendum to enable the County not to be included in a future Welsh Parliament. Kinnock had earlier been sent a petition signed by 300 of his constituents complaining that there was too much Welsh language on television. In South Wales there were very few Welsh-speaking people and therefore programmes were incomprehensible to the majority. He received many complaints from those who could only get Welsh-language programmes at peak viewing times.

As only half a million of the 2½ million population of Wales could speak Welsh, Kinnock later suggested to the Home Secretary, Roy Jenkins, that there should be a fourth television channel for Welsh-speaking programmes.

In February 1975 Kinnock resigned as Foot's PPS. The private agreement that he should only occupy this post for a year had not been widely known and there were many, especially in South Wales, who were surprised. In his letter of resignation to Foot, Kinnock wrote:

> As we anticipated, when you were good enough to appoint me, twelve months would be long enough in a position of being neither government nor fully backbench fowl. Of course, there are a few other reasons.
>
> I also want to make my opposition known on issues of mutual concern and agreement, such as the Social Contract and the future of Ebbw Vale and the valleys, without my views being attributed to my role as your parliamentary private secretary.
>
> I realise that my resignation at this time may attract the interpretation that it is a consequence of my views over the increase in the Civil List award to the Queen. My feelings on this matter, as you know, have nothing to do with my resignation.

He also stated at the time that a reason for his resignation was that he wanted to complete a book that he was preparing on the speeches of Aneurin Bevan. When interviewed, he claimed that his resignation had little to do with the closures that the Government, much to Foot's embarrassment, were making at the Ebbw Vale steelworks, stating:

> 'I resigned ... the basic reason was, that I had agreed with Michael to be his PPS for a year, and the year was up. But I publicly stated in letters to the press at the time that I thought that I could do a better job of supporting Michael Foot, who was in very difficult circumstances at the time, as his friend rather than as his PPS. Simply because the appearances given if you are a PPS are, first, that you are his master's voice, and secondly that you have a patronage debt.

Hitherto, there had been many people in South Wales who believed, with no historical justification, that Kinnock was obsessed with political advancement. In jumping off the first rung of the ladder, by his resignation, he had shown that he had a conscience, and this won him a good deal of quiet admiration. To local Welsh people his resignation was very much a feather in his cap. It also gave him a useful free hand, especially at a time when he was beginning to make a name for himself in the Labour Party. It was a curious action for a young ambitious politician. But his political ambitions, at this moment, were still unclear; he had time on his side. He was also confident that Labour would be in power for a long while in the future. Speaking to a South Wales Labour Party dinner on 28 February 1975, he said, 'We are really only just starting on the road to socialism where the workers have full control of the means of distribution and ... we will have to hold power for a long time yet.... We need to be in office for the next twenty years to make sure we secure an irreversible distribution of wealth and power.' He stated that the only means by which the newly elected Conservative leader, Margaret Thatcher, could reach Downing Street was if the Labour government failed in its election promises.

Kinnock was offered a government position by James Callaghan in 1976 as junior minister to Roy Hattersley at the Department of Prices and Consumer Affairs. Hattersley was telephoned by Callaghan who told him he would be having the troublesome Welsh MP Neil Kinnock as a junior minister. Several hours later Callaghan again telephoned to inform him that Kinnock didn't want the job. Glenys had warned Neil that Callaghan was attempting to silence him. Kinnock agreed with her and refused, for he fundamentally disagreed with Labour's policies on the economy and on devolution and he wished to be free to campaign against these, although this eventually meant that when he came to be elected party leader in 1983, he had no experience of government office whatsoever.

While Kinnock was a dedicated constituency MP, whose interests were mostly concentrated on Welsh matters, heavy industry, health and social services, he was able to lend his weight as an MP to a number of political causes. He continued to be a member of CND, and in July 1974 asked for a report to be published on an accident that had taken place at Sellafield nuclear establishment in Cumbria. Later he was to be present at an inaugural meeting of the Welsh Anti-Nuclear Alliance in Cardiff, in the spring of 1980, when he spoke of the dangers of nuclear weapons and the need for unity between the two wings of the anti-nuclear movement. He also encouraged the voice of the left in British politics. In December 1974 he presented the black American communist, Angela Davis, to a meeting at the House of Commons. He helped sponsor a meeting in Cardiff, on 10 January 1976, to increase the readership and the support for the communist newspaper *Morning Star*. When in the spring of 1978 Cumbria County Council's Library Department withdrew *Labour Weekly*, *Tribune*, and the *Morning Star* from libraries, Kinnock wrote a letter to *Labour Weekly* suggesting that Labour councillors 'for reasons of politics, education and a free press' ensure that each of these papers be bought for every library in the country.

He attended a meeting of Democratic Defence, an anti-fascist movement, in February 1975, and in November took his family on a march in Hyde Park in support of United Against Racialism. In November 1977 he hosted a press conference at the House of Commons to launch the left-wing group, the Anti-Nazi League.

For most of his career Kinnock has taken little interest in foreign policy. Although he joined a school trip to Germany when he was sixteen, it is believed that his first visit abroad was to Moscow in August 1972. This was a week-long parliamentary trip with a group of Labour MPs who visited various national and regional legislative assemblies. He did very little other foreign travelling, but in March 1978 the American State Department invited him to the United States on a three-week lecture tour. He met senators in Washington, visited slum areas in New York, car workers in Detroit, and agricultural trade unionists in California. He visited schools in Boston, and lectured to trade unionists at Harvard.

Except for his anti-Common Market campaign, during his thirteen-year parliamentary career Kinnock's interests in overseas matters took the form of protests against right-wing governments for which he had an abhorrence; he also cared deeply about the human rights issues of foreign policy. In Parliament he said that in view of the 100,000 political prisoners held in South Vietnam, aid should be halted to the government of General Thieu. He protested against the use of torture in Latin America, and signed letters to the *Guardian* concerning disappeared prisoners in Argentina, and the treatment of the Shah's political detainees in Iran. In 1974 he spoke against South Africa at the Labour Party conference. That year he also led a delegation to ask the Foreign Secretary, Jim Callaghan, to encourage the cancellation of the British Lions tour of South Africa. Kinnock then criticized Labour's Minister of Sport, Denis Howell, for going to a British Lions reception, and wrote a letter to the *Guardian* condemning the Government for permitting the British Steel Corporation to build a chrome ore plant in South Africa. In February 1975 he wrote to the South African leader Dr Vorster to ask him to release from prison the former Communist Party leader, Bram Fischer, who was dying of cancer.

Kinnock also took a great interest in protesting against the military government in Chile, which achieved power in a coup on 11 September 1973. The world's first democratically elected Marxist government, that of Salvador Allende, had taken office in 1970. Although not noticeably radical, the presence of a Marxist government in Latin America caused great concern in Washington, and the United States covertly assisted a military coup which was to topple Allende. The Labour left in Britain were furious; with some justification, particularly as the Americans let it be known that the reason for their coup was that Allende had only been elected with 38% of the popular vote: more than that achieved by several postwar British governments. Kinnock spoke about the 'poor downtrodden peasants and proletariat of Chile', and was made Secretary of the Parliamentary Chilean Group. He addressed a meeting in Trafalgar Square on behalf of the Chile Solidarity Campaign, demanding that the Government stop financial aid and the sale of arms to Chile, and he spoke on television in support of trade unionists who refused to work on aero engines bought by the Pinochet government. In April 1974 he wrote a letter to *The Times* in support of a junior minister, Eric Heffer, who had objected to the Government's supplying warships to Chile. Although it is doubtful if many of the voters in his constituency had ever heard of Chile, during the autumn 1974 general election campaign Kinnock toured his constituency using an LP of a Chilean folk group, deported by the Chilean government. In August 1975 he wrote to Senator Edward Kennedy asking for help in getting detained Britons released by Chile. He continued to be on the committee of the Chile Solidarity Campaign, but as his commitments increased during the 1970s he was seldom able to find time for meetings. At the time of the 1983 leadership election he attended a tenth anniversary concert of the movement and honoured a pledge he had given earlier to make a speech appealing for funds.

Kinnock has taken very little interest in defence policy, other than campaigning to prevent the sale of arms to autocratic right-wing governments, such as Chile. Although during the 1983 leadership campaign he claimed that Britain should scrap its nuclear deterrent and maintain strong conventional forces, he had up till then never, during his parliamentary career, voted for the defence estimates: he has usually made arrangements to speak elsewhere on these occasions. He claims that the reason for his never having voted for the defence estimates is entirely because it would mean approving funds for nuclear weapons. However, he has never even taken an interest in conventional defence. He did write a letter to the *Guardian* in December 1980 complaining of 'the political and economic torpor' of the defence budget, and spoke of government defence spending as 'obese', stating that the encouragement of arms sales abroad was making Britain a 'warfare state', and 'an arms supermarket of the dictators of the starving countries of the world', but his defence interests remained largely confined to matters of disarmament. In early 1983 he even suggested it should be Labour policy to have compulsory peace studies in secondary schools. Although never enthusiastic about defence spending, Kinnock was bitterly opposed to the Soviet invasion of Afghanistan.

A feature of Kinnock's career that is generally not appreciated is his keen interest in practical reforms of Parliament. In the tradition of Bevan and Foot he has a tremendous admiration for the House of Commons, of which he believes 'There is no cleaner or more honest national assembly anywhere in the world', but on arrival at Westminster in 1970 he had been shocked by the lack of facilities for MPs. Initially he did not have a secretary or even an office and so, like many other MPs, he was forced to write his letters to constituents sitting in the library. At one time he even used Doreen, the wife of his agent Barry Moore, as his secretary. He therefore suggested that there ought to be a system by which secretaries were employed by the House of Commons and not by MPs. From his own difficult financial time as a young member, he soon learnt the importance of MPs having adequate salaries and in March 1975 he protested at their having to suffer a 'wage freeze', claiming that the House of Commons survived on the 'generosity of bank managers'.

Kinnock had the unique distinction of being the first MP to urge the radio broadcasting of the proceedings of the House of Commons. Although MPs had several times rejected demands for Parliament to be televised either live or in edited versions, he believed there would be support for his ideas on radio broadcasting, and for many years, as a young MP, he continued his campaign for the Commons to be heard on radio. He wrote several articles for *Labour Weekly* and *Tribune* on the need for parliamentary reform, and his television appearances on BBC programmes discussing the need for better parliamentary facilities helped to get his name known to the media.

He served on various Commons select committees, most notably those on nationalized industries, but he disliked governmental committee work, seldom attending meetings. He limited himself to what interested him, rather than what needed to be done by Parliament.

Over the years the quality of Kinnock's parliamentary speeches began to improve, and it was noticeable from 1974 that he stopped making jokes in Commons debates: his questions showed a considerable and detailed knowledge of the steel and coal industries.

As has been noted earlier, Kinnock's television appearances had begun even before he was elected to Parliament. In his early years as an MP he was frequently seen on a television discussion programme hosted by Vincent Kane and broadcast on BBC Wales; his appearances on the national media began at the time of the miners' strikes. He was seen by the media as a fiery young MP with interesting ideas on parliamentary reform, who then became a leading spokesman on devolution. His ability to speak fluently off the cuff on numerous subjects was impressive: although often controversial, he could be humorous and entertaining. For the autumn 1975 series of party conferences, the BBC *Tonight* programme arranged for MPs from the various political parties to make comments on the proceedings of their rivals. Kinnock was asked to observe the Tory conference. This was to be a useful break for him, his first major solo appearance on the national media, and helped to establish him as a witty and knowledgeable commentator. His success at this conference brought him to the attention of BBC producers talent-spotting for interesting personalities for television panel shows, which led to his receiving more invitations for media appearances. What also enhanced his popularity with the media was his willingness to speak to journalists more than was usual for a Labour MP. At party conferences he would spend much of the time chatting to them.

Another important step at this time was his initiation as an amateur newspaper columnist. In June 1976 he started to write occasional articles in the 'grassrooting' series of the *Guardian*, which were read by Labour Members of Parliament and most Labour Party activists. These were easy reading, good-humoured, and never lost an opportunity to refer to his family's working-class origins. Just as Harold Wilson frequently reiterated 'As I said at the Blackpool conference', so Kinnock would scarcely ever miss an opportunity to remind his readers, or any audience, be it in Parliament, trade union meetings, or constituency gatherings, of his coal-mining origins although he himself had never worked in the mines. Indeed, like his hero Nye Bevan, Kinnock would conspicuously boast of his working-class ancestry whenever possible.

He wrote numerous articles for the newspaper *Labour Weekly*. However, in his now widening journalistic career, probably by far the most important development was writing for the socialist newspaper *Tribune*. From 1976, when he joined the paper's editorial board, until late 1979, Kinnock wrote articles almost every fortnight on subjects of current political interest. *Tribune*, which at that time was campaigning heavily against the Labour government's economic policies, had a mass circulation among party workers and his contributions greatly helped to get his name known within the Party. However, he rejected his agent Barry Moore's idea that he should broaden his writing to include political novels.

Several weeks after the successful Common Market referendum, Harold Wilson, in March 1976, announced his intention to resign as Prime Minister and leader of the Party. As it was the Parliamentary Labour Party which was to choose a leader, and thus the new Prime Minister, members of the government such as Foreign Secretary Jim Callaghan had an immediate advantage. Appearing as the elder stateman of the Labour Party, Callaghan seemed the natural successor to Wilson. There were four other contenders for the leadership: Roy Jenkins, Anthony Crosland, Denis Healey and Michael Foot.

Foot had no ambition to be leader; although he was very popular with the Parliamentary Labour Party, it was believed that he had no chance of winning. However, he was persuaded by Kinnock to fight for the leadership. A campaign team was formed and it was noted by Barbara Castle that Kinnock was one of Foot's most lively lieutenants. He made a well-publicized speech at Merthyr Tydfil, in March 1976, when he criticized the other leadership contenders without naming them: 'We are not picking an ideal father figure or a dictator. Blandness or square jaws have their uses, but neither the British people nor the Labour Government will respond to a paternal head or a strong silent sheriff.' A new leader, he claimed, 'must have the authority to select only the useful advice of civil servants and not bow to their conventionalities ... to convey to business and international opinion that democracy is in charge in Britain and to convince organized Labour that he is worthy of their full trust'. The new Labour leader, Kinnock stated, must be a comrade to his parliamentary colleagues, not a boss. However, his assessment of the kind of leader Labour needed was eventually to prove fatal, for in electioneering terms Foot's leadership from 1980 to 1983 was unfortunate. It is arguable that what Labour required was not a delegate but an aggressive leader. In the first count on 25 March, Foot was top of the list with 90 votes to Callaghan's 84, Jenkins's 56, Benn's 37, and Healey's 30. Under a first-past-the-post electoral system Foot would have won and would have been Wilson's successor as Prime Minister. However, the system in force consisted of a series of counts. In the second count Callaghan, as the 'Stop Foot' candidate, took most of Jenkins's votes. Foot got most of the Bennite votes, and a few of Jenkins's. The results of the count on 30 March were Callaghan 141 votes, Foot 133, and Healey 38. Healey was eliminated from the contest but from then on Foot stood no chance as the Healey votes went to Callaghan. At the third count in the House of Commons Grand Committee Room, on 5 April, the result was Callaghan 178 votes, Foot 137. Callaghan then made his speech to the Parliamentary Party. He said:

> So far as the past is concerned, I shall wipe the slate clean and I ask everyone else to do the same, and that includes the members of the

self-appointed groups in the House. I mean especially the Tribune Group and the Manifesto Group. None of you holds the Ark of the Covenant. The Party workers in the country demand your first loyalty to be not to your group meetings but to the Party meetings. I shall not be willing to accept a situation in which minority groups in the Parliamentary Labour Party manoeuvre in order to foist their views on the Party as a whole.

Kinnock's hero, Michael Foot, had lost but was now automatically deputy Party leader, and leader of the House, with special responsibility for devolution.

Devolution was a crucial aspect of Kinnock's career, as until the matter was resolved by a referendum in March 1979, it meant that he was in fundamental disagreement with the Labour Government. As with his opposition to the Common Market, he was firmly opposed to the idea of devolution as he believed it would only leave Wales the poorer. Kinnock was a realist who, with Labour MPs such as Eric Heffer from the deprived Midlands, feared that the devolution assemblies would draw off badly needed development funds. Kinnock showed increasing maturity and breadth of mind in putting Wales, and indeed Britain, before party. He soundly diagnosed that Plaid Cymru only had minority appeal in Wales, where historically, and especially in South Wales, the demands of internationalism had ever been stronger than those of nationalism. He believed, probably correctly, that devolution would do Britain as a whole great damage. In a powerful speech in the House of Commons as early as November 1975, he said, 'Devolution would be a monumental and irreversible step for British democracy and we cannot afford to get it wrong. The economic and social disarray of Britain and the crisis of the Western World make a diversion into constitutional wrangling a luxury which Parliament cannot afford.'

When interviewed Kinnock summarized his views on devolution as follows: 'The argument that I was trying to sustain was that the devolution proposals that had been made were bound in my view to contradict the interests of the people I was trying to represent. And it was not a general antagonism to a general principle ... but I could only see disadvantages, especially for Welsh people.'

At a Commons debate in January 1976 Kinnock criticized the

Neil Kinnock

Government's White Paper on devolution for Scotland and Wales. He claimed that the paragraph which stated: 'The Scottish and Welsh assemblies will no doubt have teething trouble ... this is well worth accepting to meet the clear popular demand' summarized the Government's philosophy on devolution which was a leap into the unknown with the mistaken belief that there was a 'popular demand' for devolution in Wales. He stated that the 1974 Labour Manifesto had said nothing about a Welsh assembly having revenue collecting powers, and demanded that a separate bill be produced for Welsh devolution.

The Government intended to get its devolution legislation on the statute-book in the 1976-77 session and prepared to start the necessary series of parliamentary debates in November 1976. In March of that year Kinnock, in a Parliamentary Question to Wilson, had asked for a referendum on devolution. Wilson had rejected this on the grounds that there was no popular demand for a referendum, not even from the Welsh TUC. Foot agreed with this point of view and stated that Kinnock's views on devolution put him in a small minority. Foot claimed that Britain had to be careful not to undermine parliamentary democracy, and should be very sparing in its use of referenda. Kinnock, however, began to increase his demands for a referendum and released a statement, which was fully supported by his constituency, which said: 'Without a referendum the great debate for which Harold Wilson called will be as meaningless as a racehorse without a winning-post.' During early August Kinnock was a prominent member of a group of Labour MPs planning a national campaign to crush the Devolution Bill if the Government did not promise a referendum. The group, which Kinnock claimed had the support of twenty-seven ministers and eighty-seven backbenchers, realized that in opposing the Devolution Bill there was a possibility of bringing down the entire Labour government, but they also believed that if the nationalist parties did not get devolution they would bring the Government down regardless. Kinnock said that if there was a referendum for the whole of Britain he would accept the result.

However, the 1976 Labour Party conference at Blackpool gave overwhelming support for the policy of devolution, urging the Government not to bother with a referendum, defeating the strongly worded anti-devolution motion, that Kinnock had helped write, by a massive 4,785,000 votes to 829,000. Although Kinnock had lost, his speech was a great personal and political triumph. There were many at the conference who disagreed with him but he was still able to achieve the greatest response and most thunderous applause of the whole debate. It was a tribute to his personal popularity and winning qualities that he could draw a standing ovation even from those who disagreed with him. He said:

> Last year ... there was such a lack of interest in both the political and industrial wings of this Movement that it was not a priority for Conference ... twelve months later, it enjoys such apparently unanimous support, such total compulsion ... as to require us to commit ourselves wholeheartedly to this irreversible constitutional change in the name of the Labour Movement ... that is the indecent haste ... the false speed of appeasement ... can we as trade unionists and Labour Party supporters put our hands on our hearts and say that we really do have the assent of the people of Britain for this irreversible and monumental constitutional change? ... instead of the harmony and the unity to which the platform refers, we will get guaranteed disharmony, disunity, conflict and competition throughout the whole of Britain.

At the Party conference, and indeed for most of the five years during which Kinnock fought against his own party's plans for devolution, he clashed bitterly in public with Michael Foot, who was the minister guiding the legislation. However, although there were these violent public disagreements, such was the strength of their comradeship that their friendship was unaffected. Indeed, as has been seen, Kinnock had earlier helped persuade Foot to stand for the leadership and had even been his most active campaigner. To Michael Foot and his wife, Neil and Glenys continued to be almost the adopted family they had never had. Although bitterly fought, devolution was no more than a passing disagreement in terms of Kinnock's relationship with Foot for, a few years later, he again persuaded Foot to fight for the leadership.

Devolution showed the crucial difference of attitude, and of character, between Foot and Kinnock. While both were determined to keep the United Kingdom together against the tide of devolution, Foot's reaction was to give in to the nationalists' demands for it because he feared that a failure to respond would only mean more disunity. He said on television that a failure to grant independence to Ireland in the nineteenth century had brought disunity: he feared that a failure to grant devolution to Wales and Scotland would produce a similar consequence, 'I don't want them to turn to violence, of course, but I think it's quite likely.' Kinnock's attitude to the prevention of disunity was the precise opposite. It was aggressively to meet those who threatened unity, the devolutionists, head on, to fight and then defeat them. He would not compromise. Unlike Foot but like Margaret Thatcher whom he despised, he was a conviction politician.

Kinnock's conviction was not to do with socialism or Labour Party policy, it was gut British thinking and common sense. For an apparent left-winger, as far as constitutional change was concerned, he was surprisingly conservative. But his innate pragmatism left him vulnerable to the charge of hypocrisy when as leader in 1983 he demanded Party unity and insisted that there was nothing wrong with Conference decisions which appeared in the Labour Manifesto. Yet only a few years earlier, in June 1976, he had justified his opposition to Conference decisions on devolution, arguing that there was no manifesto commitment that prohibited 'further debate or should prevent those with opposing conviction from campaigning and arguing in support of their views. Loyalty is a fine quality but in excess it fills political graveyards.'

Kinnock's public and almost single-handed fight against devolution was an act of immense personal and political courage. The cost of this to him was great. While he had personally been opposed to devolution for many years and had the support of his own constituency, his anti-devolutionist stance put his career at great risk. He flew in the face of the party hierarchy and upset many Labour supporters and voters in South Wales whose feelings about the matter were varied; some thinking that Labour would gain from the prestige of having granted devolution. He was even accused of being a traitor by many from the platform at the Welsh Labour Party conference in spring 1978. In a belligerent mood, Kinnock angrily defended himself: 'I flog myself up and down the country on behalf of this Party. I will not bear the charge of disloyalty.'

The trade unions in Wales were very close to Labour and

Neil Kinnock's paternal family: (*left to right*) Uncle Wilfred, Uncle Charles, his father Gordon and Uncle Harold; (*front row*) Uncle Clifford, his grandmother, Uncle William, his grandfather and Aunt Dorothy.

The house where Neil Kinnock was born, Vale View, Tredegar.

With his mother and father in Blackpool.

Neil Kinnock (*front row, second from right*) at Lewis School, Pengam.

Neil and Glenys's wedding, 25 March 1967, at Holyhead, Anglesey: (*left to right*) Gordon and Mary Kinnock, Neil, Glenys, Mr and Mrs Cyril Parry, and best man Jeff Prosser.

Dennis Skinner and Neil Kinnock in the House of Commons refusing to be summoned to the State Opening of Parliament, 3 November 1977 as a protest against the House of Lords.

As Education spokesman, Kinnock during a Labour Party Conference debate in 1981.

With his wife and children, Rachel and Stephen, at a Hyde Park demonstration against
Arts Council cuts, September 1983.

At another Hyde Park meeting, October 1983, this time the Campaign for Nuclear Disarmament.

...siting St Leonard's Hospital, Hackney, threatened with closure.

At Durham Miners' Centenary, 17 July 1983, with Glenys, Michael Foot and Tony Benn.

With Eric Heffer and Roy Hattersley (*left*) at the end of Labour's 1983 Party Conference.

Brighton, 2 October 1983: his election as the new leader of the Labour Party – (below) with Roy Hattersley and Michael Foot.

Kinnock captured the leadership with 71% of the votes.

Campaigning with Tony Benn in the Chesterfield by-election, February 1984.

favoured devolution, believing it would bring greater job security. Kinnock was criticized for ignoring the union line, and the general secretary of the Welsh TUC put Kinnock's TGWU sponsorship in question. However, when Clive Jenkins's ASTMS union let their willingness to take over Kinnock's trade union sponsorship be known, the threat was quietly abandoned. Though many trade unionists disagreed with Kinnock on the devolution issue, he won much admiration for his courage and for the style with which he put his case, even from those who disagreed with him.

Kinnock's anti-devolutionary fight made him a target for Plaid Cymru extremists. In 1977 a left-wing nationalist group published a vitriolic pamphlet entitled 'Neil Kinnock and the Anti-Taffy League', accusing him of treachery against the Welsh people. Letters were sent to the press alleging that he owned a mansion with a swimming-pool at Ascot, and that his children attended public schools. One evening when he was at his constituency house in Pontllanfraith, four drunken Welsh nationalists arrived on his doorstep, armed with a gun, and threatened to kill him. Kinnock slammed the door and telephoned the police. In 1978 the leader of Plaid Cymru, Gwynfor Evans MP, accused him in Parliament of being anti-Welsh and of supplying misleading information on the £17 million cost of providing Welsh road signs. Kinnock angrily cautioned Evans that if he made the accusation again he would sue him to bankruptcy. At a heated House of Commons debate that March Kinnock claimed that there was 'linguistic racialism' operating against non-Welsh-speaking children. Furious Welsh Nationalist MPs demanded that he send evidence of these complaints to the District Education Authority. When a large dossier of letters arrived at these offices several weeks later, it was alleged that the evidence was rigged and one of the letters was found to be from Kinnock's sister-in-law. The Education Committee then considered his allegations of 'linguistic racialism', and its report, published in July, stated that there was not the slightest evidence for the claim.

In November 1976, just as the Government were preparing to debate the Scotland and Wales devolution legislation, Kinnock organized a Commons motion with 78 Labour signatures, 67 of them from English MPs, demanding a referendum: otherwise the legislation would be destroyed. A month later the Callaghan Government agreed to a referendum but would not concede a new anti-devolutionist demand for separate bills for Scotland and Wales. Despite Kinnock's great hatred of the Conservatives, such was his intense feeling on devolution that he joined a handful of other leading Labour anti-devolutionists – Leo Abse, Donald Anderson, Fred Evans and Joan Evans – to vote with the Tories, and the Government's bill was defeated in February 1977 by 312 votes to 283. The Government then decided to try again, but this time with separate bills for Scotland and for Wales which were debated in November 1977. Kinnock and other Labour MPs helped the Conservatives move 'wrecking' amendments, one of which stated that no 'Yes' vote on a referendum would be accepted as effective unless supported by 40% of the electorate entitled to vote. As less than a general election average of 70% were expected to vote in a referendum, this effectively made it impossible for a 'Yes' vote to be approved in a Welsh referendum. Despite these efforts, Welsh devolution legislation was passed in June 1978, subject to a referendum to take place in 1979. The unofficial Labour Party 'Vote "No"' campaign, which had been formed in February 1977, led by Kinnock who was also one of its most prominent speakers, began serious operations in early 1978. That February he visited Edinburgh to campaign for the Scottish branch of the 'Vote "No"' campaign. When he later became party leader, he claimed that he was not against devolution for Scotland, which continued to be in Labour's 1983 election manifesto, but his visit in February 1978 shows this claim to be questionable.

Still fighting against the Labour Party hierarchy, Kinnock now produced a most impressive intellectual fifty-page document, 'Facts to Beat the Fantasies' – a superb argument against the devolutionists. This was compiled from figures he had procured over the years in parliamentary questions, and it successfully argued that devolution was a gamble that Wales could not afford to take. He surefootedly argued that an improvement in the social services was essential, but there was no evidence that this could be achieved with devolution. These, it will be noted, were the same cautious arguments that he had used against the Common Market. When the referendum votes were cast on 1 March 1979 the Welsh people decisively rejected devolution by 46.9% against, and only 11.9% for, a majority of nearly four to one. The voting in Kinnock's own constituency was even more dramatic at nine to one against. In Scotland the devolutionists were also humiliated.

The battle against devolution in Wales that Kinnock had successfully fought against his own Party, virtually single-handed, was a great personal victory. He believed this to have been his greatest achievement in his thirteen-year parliamentary career. It had won him much respect, especially among Welsh people, even from those who violently disagreed with him: it was another feather in his cap.

Until now Kinnock had seemed personally ambitious and keen to advance himself in the Labour Party, but he had cut himself off from the party hierarchy over devolution; hardly the action of an unscrupulous man.

Not only did Kinnock disagree with his Party over devolution, but he also disliked the 1974-9 Labour Government's economic policies. Within months of the October 1974 general election victory it became apparent that the world recession was much steeper than had been thought. In the public sector teachers, nurses, and council workers were achieving wage increases of 25-30%, in line with the conditions of the social contract; inflation was 20% and rising. To combat this the Chancellor of the Exchequer, Denis Healey, was advised by moderate Labour MPs to tighten the terms of the social contract, while the Tribunites demanded increased public spending. When sterling fell dramatically on the world markets in June, the Government established a system of limiting wage demands to 10%. With the idea, now broadly accepted, that Britain was living on borrowed time and borrowed money, the Government's March 1976 Budget stated that there would be no increases in government spending until 1979. This move was criticized by the City, whose view was that the Treasury had not gone far enough and that government spending needed to be reduced immediately. The Parliamentary Labour Party were bitterly critical of these policies, especially the Government's promise of tax cuts if the trade unions would agree to limit wage demands to 3%. Kinnock led the attack on the Government. On 11 March, with thirty-six other Labour MPs, he abstained in the voting on the

Government's economic policy. Charges of disloyalty were made against the rebels. Kinnock shrugged this off, claiming such charges had been made by party 'loyalists' in even more vitriolic language when Bevan and Wilson resigned because of the imposition of Health Service charges. He even quoted Harold Wilson's speech of resignation from the Board of Trade as an ideal definition of socialist spending priorities: 'social services should have their own priority ... they have a contribution to world peace no less real than an unattainable rearmament programme'. Speaking at a Fire Brigades' Union meeting in Torquay on 11 April, Kinnock launched a much publicized attack on the Budget, stating that the Government's 3% wage-rise limit plan was an attempt to blackmail the unions: 'This Budget codifies the beliefs of the most selfish and short-sighted saloon-bar loudmouth that income tax is the source of all evil and stagnation.... Until now, through the social contract and the £6 policy, the government has rightly been able to claim a partnership with the TUC. That partnership is now being replaced by blackmail.'

Several weeks later at a meeting in Doncaster he warned that Healey's policy would be unworkable because, 'The arguments of capitalism are carrying more weight in a Labour cabinet than are the arguments of socialism.... It seems friends are to be thanked for their loyalty and foes rewarded for their power. In the nostalgic vocabulary so fashionable now, that is not the spirit of Dunkirk, it is the tragedy of Munich.'

Kinnock continued to side with the trade unions. In November 1977 he joined fifty-eight Labour rebels who voted that the Government treat the Fire Service Unions as a special case and grant them a wage claim higher than the social contract guidelines. At the Labour Party conference that autumn he was among a chorus of left-wingers who urged Healey to produce a budget that would increase public spending. Kinnock said that the Party had to 'see that the state invests where capitalism has failed to do so. A Labour government isn't elected for inactivity, it's elected for action.' These were the words he used on 15 November 1977 during a televised party political broadcast, that took the form of a discussion between him, a trade unionist, Roy Hattersley, the Prices Secretary, and Joan Lestor. The original programme had been forty minutes of sometimes terse disagreement, and had been edited by Transport House's publicity department. In the film most of the talking was done by Hattersley, who said the Government's main concern was now unemployment. Kinnock, who was a young and visibly rather beleaguered figure at the end of the green baize table, was listened to benevolently when he demanded that Labour embark on a massive programme of public ownership, especially of North Sea oil. While both speakers were in agreement on policy, Hattersley explained to Kinnock that the country despised politicians who promised instant success. The general impression left by the programme was that Kinnock was too impatient and scarcely worth taking seriously.

It was an astonishing fact that while Kinnock was at odds with most of the policies of the Labour Government, his own personal popularity within the Party greatly increased. He was regarded by the party leadership as a troublesome left-winger. Even so, he made his name by the surprising means of being a humorist. While it would be an oversimplification to state that Kinnock won the leadership of the Labour Party by telling good jokes, this claim would not be far wrong. A natural comic, he was asked by the Tribune Group to make a collection speech at their meeting during the October 1975 Party conference. This speech, which set him on the path to Labour stardom, was a hilarious flight of oratory and it brought the house down. Barbara Castle noted in her diary that it was the funniest collection speech she had ever heard, and that Kinnock was a 'great find' for the Labour Party. A year later, at the Blackpool conference, when only thirty-six, he was able to make his first attempt at election to the Labour National Executive Committee. The institution of the annual Party conference, in the Labour Party, is far more important than is generally realized, as its earnest deliberations and resolutions take on the authority of Scripture. A politician who can make himself known in the meritocracy of public speaking there, can be a major force in the Party. While Kinnock had made himself personally and widely liked by his humorous 1975 Tribune speech, he denies that his attempt at election to the NEC was because he was ambitious. Having achieved a credible personal fan club in the party, he was starting to storm the foothills of the Labour leadership. He claims that he stood for the NEC, because of the large number of people in various places in the country who said that I should stand for the NEC. And I thought that there was a specific job to be done. The job to be done at the time ... seemed to me to be one of political organization, and education, and I thought that the National Executive Committee should play a leading part in that. That was the basis on which I stood.

At the 1976 Blackpool conference Kinnock, having won over many of the constituency parties at his public speaking meetings during the year, got a staggering 155,000 votes at his first attempt to get elected to the NEC. Neil and Glenys were surprised and astounded to get so many votes at the first attempt: they were also thrilled as the vote was clearly something that could be built on and it could only be a matter of two or three years before Kinnock would get elected. The 1976 vote was also more significant than it appeared at the time because, during that conference, Kinnock had made a superb blistering attack on Labour's devolution policy, proving that it was possible to publicly defy the Party leadership and still advance in popularity. As Kinnock and his election agent, Barry Moore, well knew, there were many delegates, as there still are now, who would go the party conference with no idea for whom they were going to vote. Kinnock's infectious sense of humour endeared him to many delegates, and his brilliant speeches, irrespective of their content, achieved wonders. The fact that he was a working-class lad who told humorous jokes about the Tories was an absolutely crucial feature in his rise to power. Many in the Labour Party regarded him as a friend who could be trusted, who could be relied and depended upon, a feeling which was heightened by his ability to make them laugh. As his reputation for being a bit of a comic spread from Parliament to the constituency parties, he was invited to join the comedy team who did satirical shows at conferences. At the 1977 Brighton conference Kinnock's star presence in the review entitled 'End of the Peers Show' meant that every ticket was sold. This helped him to increase his number of NEC votes to 244,000. The Brighton vote meant that he was in the 'line of succession' for the NEC and within striking distance of a chance of election in 1978. Glenys, who was also his campaign manager, was convinced his increased number of votes had been helped by his intensive public speaking and now frequent television appearances.

Kinnock's left-wing stance had been crucial for winning him the constituency votes for the NEC, but it was the votes of the Labour right-wingers that brought him so near to election. The Labour Party was now visibly beginning to fragment into a variety of warring tribes, one of which, the recently established centre right 'Campaign for Labour Victory', led by personalities such as Shirley Williams, Dr David Owen, and William Rogers, recommended constituencies to use one of their seven votes for Kinnock because they thought he represented the 'respectable left'. The reason for Kinnock's respectability with the right at that stage, was the humour of his speeches, for wit was a rare feature amongst left-wingers. This was not only useful for his election bid for the NEC but later, in 1983, when he made his successful bid for the leadership, it was his credibility to those on the right of the Parliamentary Party that made his challenge seem plausible.

Kinnock now proceeded to increase his tempo. More speeches were delivered with greater panache: their contents were harsher and more acerbic, homing in on their targets with greater directness.

He associated middle-class traditions with the Tory Party and made many personal attacks on the Conservative old guard, such as William Whitelaw, Julian Amery, and Sir Keith Joseph. In June 1979 he launched an attack on the British Ambassador to Washington, Sir Nicholas Henderson, who had leaked to the press a Foreign Office paper which stated that Britain was only a third-rank power. Kinnock criticized the Ambassador for his 'public-school image' and 'cheap saloon-bar jingoism': 'He is the product of his background and his opinions are the sort you can hear over the cocktails anywhere. They are the views of what I call fifth-column patriots. They have the welfare of the country at heart, but they are so often portraying Britain as shabby and downtrodden that it becomes accepted abroad.'

Many of his attacks were concentrated on middle-class institutions. On numerous occasions he objected to the honours system and suggested that there should just be a 'Parliamentary Services Medal'. He also actively campaigned for the abolition of the House of Lords. In November 1976 he wrote an article in *Tribune* which stated: 'The House of Lords must go, not be reformed, not be replaced, not be reborn ... just closed down, abolished, finished. ... Reform would simply give an unwarranted democratic legitimacy to a body that has no place in an elective, multi-party parliamentary system of representation.' He described the ancestors of the House of Lords as a 'tribe of brigands, muggers, bribers, and gangsters who robbed, murdered or cheated their way to privileges in earlier centuries'. When the NEC recommended the abolition of the Lords in January 1977, Kinnock said at the time that if the Government spent a year on abolishing the Lords 'democracy would be profitably advanced', and was saddened that abolition was not included in Labour's manifesto for the 1979 general election.

He was much criticized for his attacks on the Royal Family at the time of the Queen's Silver Jubilee. In an article that he wrote for the *Guardian* he claimed that watching the 1953 coronation had made him feel sick, and that was a reaction which he said 'has been with me ever since'. While most Labour MPs kept a dignified silence on the matter of the civil list, Kinnock voted against it in 1975, and stated in Parliament that as the Queen was one of the wealthiest women in the world, a Crown Department should be established to clear the 'mists that surround the whole question of the Queen's personal and private wealth'. He later referred to the Duke of Edinburgh as 'a retired naval officer without visible means of support', and in July 1977 appeared on television to object to Government plans to give the Queen several BAC 1/11 aircraft as a Jubilee present. The Silver Jubilee occurred during a time of heavy wage restraint in the public sector and a controversial strike by the Fire Service. This added to Kinnock's resentment against the monarchy. On 3 November 1977 he refused to be summoned to hear the Queen's speech at the State opening of Parliament. A tabloid newspaper published a picture of Kinnock sitting in the deserted House of Commons when the other MPs had gone to listen to Her Majesty's speech. He later sulkily demanded to know the cost to public funds of the State opening of Parliament: the answer was £12,000.

Kinnock received so many letters of criticism from the public after this that he temporarily stopped his attacks on the Royal Family. In his own constituency guests watched with horror when at a 1981 civic dinner Glenys and Neil stood for the loyal toast to the Queen but refused to touch their drinks.

When asked in October 1983 if he objected to the monarchy as an institution he replied, 'Yes. I suppose it is more to do with the institution of inheritance, rather than the British monarchy. And I think, like a lot of British people, my view of the monarchy is coloured by the absence of any credible or preferable alternatives.' During the 1983 leadership election he was asked by David Frost on TV-am if the role of the Royal Family would change with Kinnock as Prime Minister. He replied:

> Oh, not the Royal Family. There is no reason why it should, is there? Er, I mean, apart from the fact that there has to be a headship of state. The Royal Family makes a particular subscription [contribution] and responds to the British temperament. I mean, there is some resentment as to the tailback of associates with the Royal Family, but [as to] the immediate members of the Royal Family, as well, I don't think there is any significant resentment.

As the 1978 Labour Party conference approached, Kinnock did not think much of his chances of election to the NEC because he would be fighting such well-established figures as Foot, Mikardo, Hamilton, and Heffer. Kinnock told his local paper that he thought the NEC would be as before, 'But I am prepared to keep on working for membership until I succeed. I am very interested in reforming the Labour Party. There are several reforms which I believe to be vital.' It was with great irony that at the start of this Party conference, on 2 October 1978, precisely five years before the 1983 leadership election, the *Guardian* published articles by Hattersley and Kinnock. Hattersley complained that the Labour Party had been taken over by thinkers rather than evangelists: Kinnock provided advice to delegates about where to find the best pubs. Later Kinnock obtained 274,000 votes, and just nine years after being nominated as an MP, and at the age of only thirty-six, achieved another political ambition and won a place on the NEC. He went to a Blackpool wine bar for a champagne celebration with some political cronies including the Clydeside shipbuilders' union leader and former Communist, Jimmy Reid. Kinnock said he hoped his election would provide a foundation for introducing 'industrial democracy' into the Parliamentary Labour Party.

Although it was the votes of the Labour right that had helped Kinnock win a place on the NEC, he knew that his greatest strength came from the grassroots constituency workers on the left. During a speech to Conference he made a controversial attack on a senior moderate, former Labour deputy leader, Roy Jenkins. Referring to the leadership election campaign of 1976, he said:

> There was among the candidates, for instance, one Roy Jenkins – Taffy as we used to call him [laughter]. And there is a story told – it is a bit of propaganda that was put about, but I think it illustrates the point of the leadership election very adequately – about an elderly Yorkshire member who was sitting in the room, and was approached by one of Roy's acolytes – sorry, I mean supporters – and asked: 'Will you be voting for Roy Jenkins?' And the Yorkshire member said: 'No lad, we're all Labour here'. [laughter]

This went down well with the party workers, but several newspapers, including the popular tabloid the *Sun*, said that his remarks were an unwarranted and gratuitous sneer and that he had made a fool of himself. But as a leading left-winger and a darling of party conferences, he continued to improve his party standing. In November he was elected chairman of the House of Commons group of Welsh Labour MPs.

Kinnock's political thinking has always been honed by his feelings on class and on the trade unions. His poor, hard-working Welsh family environment has imbued him with a deep resentment against the middle classes. He considers his Welsh background a great political advantage and in his newspaper articles, at conferences, and on television, he has never lost an opportunity to remind audiences of his humble origins. Much of his popularity among the constituency parties can be accounted for by this working-class image, which gave him an aura of trustworthyness and stability; an additional strength was that he did not have a working-class accent. He has the self-assurance and articulation of the middle classes, and his pleasant sense of humour means that they do not feel threatened by his ideas. As a meritocrat who has succeeded entirely by his own efforts, Kinnock has a great hatred of ancestor worship and inherited privilege. This also means a prudish, inverted snobbery, and a puritanical dislike of formality. However, his ideas on class have often been old-fashioned, and politically have not taken account of the growing new middle-class electorate. Although he criticized the middle classes, it was these votes that Labour needed in order to win general elections.

Kinnock's stated opposition to what he considers to be ancestor worship is curious, as he is himself obsessed with the old traditions of the trade unions and his own working-class origins. Loyalty to the trade unions had been a family tradition. In Parliament he has campaigned actively for the trade unions, most notably from the time of the 1973 miners' strike. Among trade union leaders his loyalty and dedication to unions and the Labour Party have been greatly admired; he has often been invited to speak at trade union conferences. While he was pleased to help the trade unions, he also knew of their usefulness to his career. What made Kinnock so popular at conferences was that while his speeches were humorous, he could produce detailed and modern arguments, as he deliberately kept himself informed about trade union legislation. However, he has a tendency to romanticize his working-class origins, and in 1977 established a meeting in Tredegar that attracted a crowd of 1,000 to celebrate an 1839 Chartist march. Such was his enthusiasm for working-class history that he did not see that this was also ancestor worship.

5 · Civil War

In the 1970s there were no senior Labour public speakers who could attract the millions of voters that Labour needed to win general elections. Foot was a brilliant House of Commons debater and could delight audiences of the party faithful, but in electoral terms was a liability. It was a famous speech that Kinnock made at the 1979 Party conference that established him as a major Labour speaker. He then served on the NEC Press and Publicity Committee, and was asked to write the official Labour handbook on public speaking. Entitled 'How to Speak in Public', this was published in February 1980, and consisted of common-sense hints, amusingly written, and illustrated with cartoons. He stated in the pamphlet that it was essential for the Labour Party to present itself well: 'Our best arguments can fail and our strongest message be lost by poor presentation. The new members which we seek will not join us if they cannot understand us and will not remain if we bore them by being ineffectual, irresolute or inarticulate.' At Conservative Party speaking classes pupils are taught the importance of writing a speech at least a week in advance, learning it by heart, and practising the precise timing of jokes. Pupils at the speaking classes are told that Michael Heseltine, the star performer at Tory Party conferences, prepares and writes his main speeches at least a week beforehand. However, what has previously never been known is that Kinnock, who is the finest Labour orator since Bevan, scarcely ever writes or even prepares a speech. When he goes to speak at a meeting he will have only the most general idea of the subject of his speech. It will often not be until he is at the meeting and on the platform, when he will judge the mood of the audience, or what he describes as 'smell an audience', that he begins to formulate his ideas, taking a scrap of paper and merely jotting down single words at random. He will use these few jottings to help his memory, otherwise relying on his remarkable gift of speech. This lack of speech preparation is no insult to his audience, it is just that he is such an accomplished public debater, that it is simply not necessary. Kinnock's greatest power as a charismatic vote winner is that even people who thought his views absurd admire his oratory. He is such a courageous, confident, and powerful performer that he can go to meetings and attack the very people who have invited him, and still be applauded.

Kinnock's great natural talents meant that the more the people got to know him the better they liked him. Publicity was essential for getting his name known, and as he could deliver quick-witted ripostes he was often asked by journalists for quotations. However, Glenys believed that Neil was naïve about the press, though his attitude was that the media were going to write their stories, and so it was best to be approachable. A good press has been an essential factor in Kinnock's meteoric career: unique among the Party's left-wingers, before he was elected leader, he had never had a bad word written of him. He won much respect for his fundamental decency and sense of humour. He hated parliamentary gossip, listening to none and telling none: he has rarely been known to speak ill of Labour Party members and other than for his speaking tours, has never kept a diary.

However, while Kinnock could get thunderous applause at party conferences, trade union meetings and constituency meetings, he was never a notable speaker in the House of Commons. He never seemed to get over his awe of Parliament. In November 1974 he said that he still trembled every time he debated in the House, no matter how frequently he spoke. In a book published in 1981 he was listed as an even more popular parliamentary debater than Enoch Powell, Edward Heath, or Michael Foot. This seems unlikely. Even in the early 1980s, when he was a shadow Education Minister, MPs considered him a sincere but rather irresponsible parliamentary clown, and a parliamentary lightweight.

As noted earlier, Kinnock had made a name for himself on television during the mid 1970s because of his anti-devolution campaign. He was soon regarded by producers as the ideal 'stage left-winger'; in 1976, while still an unknown MP, he appeared on

BBC television no less than seventeen times, discussing a whole range of issues such as the social contract, MPs' salaries, and parliamentary reform. What is not generally realized is that Kinnock was an even greater success on radio. In 1977 he spoke on BBC radio on twenty-four occasions. Devolution was the main subject of discussion, but he was asked to make contributions to programmes on a wide variety of subjects such as British Steel, the Tribune Group and economic policy. With his knowledge of broadcasting he was appointed a member of the BBC General Advisory Council in 1977. His wit and tremendous sense of humour soon made him a popular guest on chat shows. From the summer of 1977 he continued to be a guest every few months on the BBC radio programme *Any Questions*, and was also frequently on *Quote ... Unquote* and the *Jimmy Young Programme*. Party conferences made Kinnock known to the constituency Labour parties and trade unions but it was his appearances on television that made him known to the mass British electorate. He was a natural television performer, and had the advantage of a flat provincial Welsh accent that offended no one. He was frequently on the popular discussion programme *Question Time*, and often appeared on *Newsnight* and *Nationwide*. In 1980 he appeared on BBC television on fifty-five occasions, and even so had to turn down many invitations, and found his popularity something of an embarrassment among his colleagues. Although Kinnock was still a young and relatively unknown MP, he was appearing on television more often in a month than most MPs could hope for in their entire parliamentary careers.

In the late 1970s the Party's frail majority in Parliament was further reduced when its main election-night spokesman, Labour MP Brian Walden, resigned to take a lucrative job as a television presenter. Kinnock, who at this time had also been offered a job as a television presenter but dismissed it with the contempt that it deserved, thereafter was one of Labour's main television personalities. He frequently appeared on Election Special programmes, and began to be considered as the television voice of the Labour Party.

He liked his television appearances to show his sincere, pipe-smoking, Welsh-teacher, family-man image but there was a ruthless streak in his character that was less evident. Each television appearance would bring a flurry of letters to his tiny office at the

House of Commons, inviting him to speak. While most politicians would consign these to the waste-paper basket, Kinnock would try to attend each one. His justification for this was that he had always believed it was the duty of Labour MPs to speak at as many public meetings as possible. However, as he well knew that most MPs were no good at this, his argument was largely a justification for his own public speaking. Glenys felt that Neil was like a woman with ten children who did not know how to use the word 'no'. His public-speaking tours caused the family much hardship, and although he was unceasingly loyal, they strained his marriage. He would speak in his constituency most weekends, and around the country during the week both in the afternoon and in the evening.

Kinnock would attend meetings wherever he was asked, even in hopeless constituencies where people would never vote Labour in a million years. Barry Moore said that he was 'an agent's night-mare', for in his enthusiasm to help Labour he often wasted his talents, exhausting himself to no avail. This frenzied schedule eventually led him to make rushed and unprepared speeches which showed the more sinister growth of his belief that what was good for Neil Kinnock was good for the Labour Party, and what was good for the Labour Party was also good for Neil Kinnock. In 1979 he drove 23,000 miles in his red Austin Princess, making a host of public-speaking trips. When he was appointed shadow Education Minister that year, he started to make a more disciplined and planned approach, often travelling by rail, using sleeping-cars, on what he described as 'mini-tours', visiting schools and colleges in the afternoon and constituencies in the evening. Most politicians would have a set speech that would be delivered at each meeting. Kinnock would however not do this. Often he would arrive at a meeting and, not even bothering with a few words on a scrap of paper, would just start talking. In his time as shadow Education Minister his speaking diaries show that he made a phenomenal one hundred such mini tours every year. This was undoubtedly a great morale raiser to the party activists in the constituencies; it also meant he collected numerous IOUs that helped to increase his vote on the NEC and, most important, enabled him to win the leadership. He cultivated a wide variety of constituencies through-out the country, particularly in the London area. It was his evident popularity with these constituency parties that first alerted journalists to the idea that he might, sometime, become a future leader. In Fleet Street in early 1980 journalists learnt that the three main speakers the constituencies were asking for from Labour Party headquarters were Benn, Hattersley, and Kinnock.

In the summer of 1980 Neil and Glenys moved with the family from Dysart Avenue, Kingston-on-Thames, to a comfortable Victorian semi-detached house in Ealing which they had bought for £42,000. The main reason for the move was that the Kinnocks were worried about the education of their children, as the standard of teaching in the schools in Kingston was of such poor quality. Several Conservative newspapers claimed at the time that Kinnock had moved to Ealing to send his children to grammar schools. There was no truth whatsoever in this story, and the Kinnock children resumed their comprehensive-school education in Ealing. They also decided on Ealing because it was easier for commuting to Parliament, near to the M4 and Paddington station, which Kinnock used for his frequent trips to the constituency. They were now visibly beginning to change their lifestyle. The miner's son and the signalman's daughter now had a week-end cottage in his constituency and a town house in a smart London suburb. They had acquired the aspirations of the middle classes, and the material possessions of a two-car family, with a pool table, a video, and trips abroad. However, Kinnock acknowledged that his family were of the newly-middled class. As a meritocrat, he had deserved success and had worked hard. Other than politics, the Kinnocks' main intellectual interests were music and the theatre. Neil would take Glenys to a production every few weeks, he was a director of the Theatre Company (England) Ltd, and had campaigned for financial help to the theatres.

In 1977, while the Kinnocks were still living in Kingston, Neil joined the London Welsh Rugby Club. His son was in the under-elevens mini rugby team, and the club asked him (he often refereed childrens' soccer matches) if he would like to coach a mini rugby team. While he had been an enthusiastic rugby player at University, he had never been much good, and was not considered of proficient standard to be in the senior London Welsh teams. However, he was to prove a highly capable coach, and very popular. He worked hard and gave up his own time for nothing to be at the field each Sunday morning in the muck and the mud. Professionally-trained coaches who watched him preparing his squad were impressed by his knowledge and his mini rugby team were successful at winning matches. There was no question of Kinnock doing the coaching as a publicity stunt as virtually no one at the rugby club knew he was an MP. It was only years later that he realized the advantage of his rugby image, and after being elected Labour leader wrote a chapter for a humorous rugby book. As a great enthusiast, he attempted to have parliamentary legislation passed to assist the sport. At the 1978 Wales v. England match he had been infuriated at the large number of tickets being sold by touts, and tabled a Commons motion asking rugby international sides to ensure that tickets were only distributed to 'dedicated, knowledgeable, and enthusiastic supporters'. In February 1979 he sponsored a private member's Sale of Tickets Bill under the ten-minute rule, that would have made it illegal, with a £500 fine, for agencies to sell tickets for theatres, concerts, and sports grounds. He said in 1979 that if he resigned from politics the only job he would like to have would be managing the Wales international team.

The success of Kinnock's election to the NEC at the 1978 Party conference was not reflected in the electoral fortunes of the Labour Party which were growing desperate. Foot had advised Prime Minister Callaghan to order an autumn general election, but Callaghan, taking Wilson's advice, and believing that Labour could achieve a further round of wage restraint with the trade unions, appeared on television to state that there would be no general election. While trade union leaders had agreed with Callaghan's plea for this further round, this was rejected by the union membership. The 'winter of discontent' began in January 1979 with a strike by transport and public service workers, rubbish accumulated in the streets, and dead were unburied, and there was much public bitterness. Labour's claim that they were the only party that could control the unions was seen to be incorrect. Kinnock's own reaction was, as usual, to support the side of the trade unions. He wrote a letter to the *Guardian* in February urging the media to stop its 'gross anti-union bias' that could do the trade unions great harm. In the House of Commons he stated that the sight of Fleet

Street rubbing its hands with glee at the Labour Government's misfortunes with the unions made the free press seem like that of the Nazi, Dr Goebbels.

On 1 March 1979 Wales and Scotland rejected devolution in a referendum; and nationalist parties now had no reason to support the Government. Foot, as Leader of the House, had been trying to find a means of keeping the Government in office, and the Plaid Cymru MPs were offered, for their continuing support, legislation to give compensation for slate quarry workers suffering from pneumoconiosis. Kinnock was furious at the granting of this to Plaid Cymru, as the Pneumoconiosis Act had been fought for by the trade unions and Labour Party in North Wales in years of campaigning. However, on 28 March the Government were defeated on a Conservative motion of no confidence by 311 votes to 310 and preparations were made for a general election.

Although still politically unknown to the public, Kinnock, as a member of the NEC, was able to take a minor part in planning Labour's election strategy. In early April he attended an NEC and cabinet Clause 5 council-of-war meeting at Downing Street. Although he was now thirty-seven, and had been an MP for nine years, unlike other MPs of similar age who had accepted junior ministries, Kinnock had rarely been to Downing Street. As a Labour Party celebrity, he was asked to write a series of features for *Tribune* which appeared each week during the election campaign under the heading 'Neil Kinnock's Election Diary'. Earlier, in April, he had collaborated on a pamphlet 'Why Vote Labour?' that attempted to 'put the common-sense case for socialism to the electorate'. While he did not neglect his own constituency, he made a punishing series of visits to twenty-eight other constituencies during the campaign. This meant a gruelling itinerary and much night-time travelling. Having done some electioneering in London, Neil and Glenys went to Merseyside and South Lancashire, encouraging party workers, canvassing, and speaking. That week ended unfortunately when the car broke down while travelling home at 3 a.m. on a Friday morning. In Kinnock's own constituency journalists campaigning with him were amazed by his energy and obvious pleasure at meeting people and fighting for the Labour Party.

The Thatcher-led Conservative Party fought the 1979 general election on a popularist programme of law and order, a free vote on hanging, the curbing of union power, higher defence spending, selling council houses, government spending cuts, a parents' charter, and the halting of further comprehensive schools. Kinnock, contesting his fourth general election, had as usual done well in his constituency, where he was by now a local hero. Of a total possible electorate of 50,708, he won 28,794 votes, while the Conservative candidate only achieved 8,358; Plaid Cymru 2,648; and the Ecology Party 556. Kinnock thus had a majority of 20,436. In the country as a whole Labour were defeated, achieving only 36.9% of the vote, and the Conservative Party swept to power. The result was grim news for Labour as it was the biggest recorded swing against a government in power since the war, while Labour's percentage of the vote was its lowest since 1931.

In early 1979, with Labour now in opposition, the Parliamentary Labour Party held elections for the twelve places in the shadow cabinet. Kinnock was fourteenth, polling seventy-nine votes, just a few less than fellow-Tribunite MP Eric Heffer, who had refused a job as a shadow minister. This result again showed that Kinnock was more popular in the party as a whole than he was respected for his abilities amongst his parliamentary colleagues. As the result of the shadow cabinet election was not binding upon Callaghan, as Party leader, Michael Foot persuaded him to appoint Kinnock to a shadow cabinet job. Kinnock was undoubtedly ready for promotion and he now had an additionally good chance of getting a job because leader Callaghan was supposedly keen to promote Welsh MPs. Callaghan agreed with Foot, and when the shadow cabinet was formed on the evening of 17 June, precisely nine years since he had been elected to the House of Commons, Neil Kinnock was named as shadow Education spokesman. He was to have this job for four years, until the autumn 1983 leadership election.

Although he received no increase in his parliamentary salary for being on the shadow cabinet, and it involved much additional work, it was an opportunity to influence policy and a job that he could not possibly refuse. With no grounding as a junior minister in government, and only hours from being given his portfolio, he had to denounce the effect of Budget spending cuts on education when the Commons debated the Tories' new education legislation. Having been appointed to the shadow cabinet but not elected to it by the Parliamentary Labour Party meant that he could still oppose Callaghan on the NEC as much as he wished. In career terms this was the most important event to happen to Kinnock since joining the NEC a few months earlier, second only to being elected to Parliament in 1970.

When he was given his shadow cabinet job, he was alleged in educational newspapers to know nothing about education. This was inaccurate. Since he had become an MP, Glenys, who taught at a comprehensive school, had kept him up to date on educational developments. He had spoken on educational matters in Parliament, most notably during the debate on Labour's 1976 education legislation. As early as December 1970 he had asked the then Education Secretary, Margaret Thatcher, parliamentary questions on school meals, polytechnics, and student loans. During his time as a WEA lecturer he had discovered that there were still in Britain as many as one million illiterate adults. In Parliament he launched a campaign to persuade the Government to take note of the findings of the Russell Report on adult education and reduce the level of illiteracy. In August 1976 he had fought, unsuccessfully, to get an adjournment debate on youth unemployment. Kinnock disagreed with Conservative plans to make education authorities publish a prospectus. As he jokingly said in the House of Commons, they might have to give such information as 'fourteen of our fifth-form girls were pregnant at the age of fifteen'.

Education was a perfect job for Kinnock: he was well-informed on the subject; it also enabled him to give vent to his passionate socialism. Surprisingly, this was the first position of governmental-style responsibility that he had had since his time as president of the Students' Union at Cardiff. It is therefore interesting to consider how he performed his task, as a shadow minister.

As he had at Cardiff, he demonstrated a tendency to be a dictator, to build constitutional changes around the personality of Neil Kinnock. Though a hard-working and popular meritocrat, Kinnock's interests were narrow and he appeared to be only an average politician who temperamentally lacked endurance. He loved the Stalinist idea of 'centralism', and was determined a new Labour government would introduce a radical mechanism to co-ordinate agencies involved in education and employment. Of his centralist instincts he said, 'I for one personally favour the concept of a single department which could bring government responsibility for education into the eighties but I recognize the difficulties involved.' Indeed, he boiled this down to an idea for a new Department of Education, Training and Leisure. He also said he wanted to see a core curriculum for schools, but several years later he publicly denounced this whole idea.

He hated the ministerial side of the job that meant reading many educational papers and documents. Despite his knowledge of the subject, it took him a long time to read himself into the education portfolio: it was several months before he was able to offer concrete ideas for Labour's education policy. This persistent avoidance of the need to grow up and accept the practical burdens of ministerial life continued to be a characteristic of Kinnock's until he became leader. More a man of action than a plodding scholar, he dashed about the country to speak at as many educational conferences as he could, where he did more talking than listening; this was later to show in the idealistic and theoretical education policy he gradually formulated. He was keener on the active but somewhat hopeless campaigning element of his education duties, speaking at numerous demonstrations against government cuts, than he was at learning about conditions at the chalk face.

He established several working groups to formulate policies to put to the Labour Party conference, for ratification in a general Charter for Educational Development that would in effect be a draft White Paper on education for a new Labour government. He religiously chaired the meetings of his Education Committee and the various working parties. These had been required by a resolution passed at the 1979 Party conference to consult with a far-left pressure group known as the Socialist Educational Association (SEA). Kinnock spoke at many SEA meetings and arranged a series of SEA and Labour Party meetings. Although, with his socialist banter, he was the star at such gatherings, he ignored the advice of many other socialist pressure groups, most notably the teachers, and as a result his policy was remote and impracticable. His failure to achieve a wider consensus made his education policy one of the least voteworthy sections of Labour's manifesto for the 1983 general election.

However, although Kinnock might have been wrong, he had the self-confidence and the moral fibre not deliberately to try to make himself popular; he showed courage in the formulation of his policy, and mature signs of pragmatism. For instance, he was personally enthusiastic about adult education, but even so he stated that this was not a priority in Labour's education programme; invited to attend a NUT conference of Welsh teachers in April 1980, he told them that the standard of their teaching was mediocre. He suggested that a British professional teachers' council should be established to get rid of incompetent teachers.

Kinnock considered the cornerstone of Labour's educational policy to be its youth training programme. When he was a junior MP, as long ago as 1975, he had suggested that every youngster between the ages of sixteen and twenty-one should have the status of 'trainee' and be given a basic youth wage. When he was shadow Education Minister, he several times reiterated the need for a universal system of education and training for 16–19-year-olds, and in February 1981 these ideas of his were eventually published as a discussion paper entitled '16–19 Learning for Life'. Kinnock's plans were to scrap sixth-form education and A-levels, and have just vocational tertiary colleges that would require no academic entrance qualifications. Students would enter Oxford or Cambridge without A-levels. Although sincere, fundamentally decent and well meaning with a genuine concern to help the young and unemployed, his educational schemes did seem theoretical and impractical. He said, 'The obsession with academic learning which is central to British capitalism's view of education has divided generations with its categories of success and failure that are generally inaccurate and usually irrelevant to our social and economic needs.' Each 'trainee' would be given £20 per week pocket money by the state, whether they were in work, education or training. The programme would be administered along Kinnock's centralist lines by an interdepartmental board and a specially appointed minister. The total cost of the scheme he estimated to be at least £1.6 billion. This was rather bewildering economics, and it was difficult to believe that his ideas on devolution and the simplicity of his education policy could be the work of the same person. Kinnock launched this scheme with a party political broadcast which featured some skinheads persuasively arguing why they should be given £20 per week pocket money. He said of Labour government financing for the scheme, 'The money will come from oil revenues, the windfall profits of banks, and savings from a reflated economy.'

Up to the time of the 1979 general election Kinnock was still virtually unknown to most of the public. But as shadow Education Minister he gained notoriety as the scourge of private education. An early action of the Thatcher government was to pass legislation to stop education authorities forcing grammar schools to become comprehensives. As shadow spokesman, Kinnock fought against this legislation and promised that a new Labour government would 'secure speedy adherence' to the comprehensive school system. In July 1980 he published a much-leaked discussion document, 'Private Schools', the most detailed study of the public schools Labour had ever made. In the pamphlet Kinnock envisaged waves of legislation to eliminate private education over a ten-year period. The discussion paper recommended that a new Labour government, immediately on taking office, would introduce a short bill to end the Assisted Places Scheme and prevent local authorities buying places in private schools for bright pupils. Several months later it would pass a more detailed Education Act to prohibit private schools from charging fees, giving the Education Secretary and local authorities power to take into public ownership those private schools which they required for community purposes. The new Education Act would also establish a national agency to ensure that private schools were used for the education of a wider sector of the population. Kinnock's policy for scrapping private education, which also included imposing VAT on private school fees, won a huge majority of 7,000,000 votes to 7,000 at the 1980 Party conference, and thus automatically became Labour Party policy.

Although at the time the paper had been for discussion only, Kinnock received much press vilification for his plans to legislate against private education. It was alleged that his campaign against the public schools was based on his own hatred of the middle

classes. There was some evidence to support this in various interviews that he gave at the time. He said, with glee, that he was
looking forward to the debates in the House of Commons when
Labour was in power and to passing legislation to abolish the public
schools. 'It will be Armageddon,' he said. 'I think the public school
system is the last redoubt of the Establishment. It is the citadel to
which . . . the middle classes would cling most defiantly.' He stated
that the private schools 'are the very cement in the wall that divide
British society', and suggested that Bradfield College, a 130-year-
old public school, should be made into a camp for Vietnamese
refugees. When invited to visit the school he said 'I am not going
to subscribe to a political stunt for the Young Conservatives'.

Kinnock had what his supporters describe as a unique and
Messiah-like 'loaves and fishes' gift to make plenty from nothing.
His lively and charismatic personality made the usually boring
subject of education policy a success within the Labour Party. Yet,
if he were to use the style of his education policies in Labour's
policies generally, as leader, Labour would never again win a
general election. As leader, Kinnock himself believes that there is
nothing wrong with Labour's policies, it is just that the public
don't understand them. However, many knowledgeable and intelligent people disliked his schemes and many informed observers
doubted if they were even practicable. *The Times Educational
Supplement* was sceptical about Labour's plans and doubted their
realism, remembering that while Labour was in office in 1968 the
Party conference had passed a resolution demanding the abolition
of public schools, but nothing had happened. Roy Hattersley, when
shadow Education Minister, had promised to abolish the public
schools, but when Labour was again in office in 1974 the commitment vanished. When Kinnock, the great centralist, produced a
controversial scheme for national government to finance virtually
every part of education spending, he was fiercely attacked by
Labour councillors. His education policies were as remote and
obsolete as Labour itself was to be under the leadership of Michael
Foot, reflecting its increasingly isolated beliefs. Kinnock was too
concerned with useless training schemes and the politics of class
warfare, and there was no evidence of concern for quality or
academic achievement: he was obsessed with proliferating medioc-

rity, unwilling or unable to lead through excellence. Parents were increasingly becoming concerned with academic standards in schools, and indeed a crucial factor of the Conservative election success in 1979 had been the idea of a Parents' Charter. Even though there was a growing public disillusionment with comprehensive schooling, Kinnock pledged to restore that sacred Labour cow. The clearest case of a generally widespread lack of sympathy for his policies was among the teachers themselves. Surveys showed that 89% of teachers in the maintained sector did not want private schooling ended. While Kinnock had warned in 1982 that teachers voting Tory at a general election would be like 'mice voting for cats', a survey done by *The Times Educational Supplement* showed that apart from those who intended to vote SDP, a plurality of teachers, 44%, planned to vote Conservative.

Although Kinnock's education policies, formulated during his four years as a senior Labour shadow minister, were essentially impractical and evoked little sympathy from the British electorate, his attacks on middle-class institutions were to win him much party popularity. His speech at the Labour Party conference on 4 October 1979 was to prove the hitherto most momentous of his career, and put him firmly on the road to Labour stardom. As yet still unknown to the public, he had the advantage of being one of the few members of the shadow cabinet not associated with Labour's recent June 1979 general election defeat. The speeches that Thursday morning at the conference had been unusually tedious, and this persisted during the education debate. Kinnock, who had to give his first speech to the conference from the platform, as a member of the shadow cabinet, had taken the unusual step of preparing a speech. Moments before he was due to appear on the rostrum he lost his notes: unknown to the audience, the speech was entirely spontaneous. 'I had some words scribbled down on a piece of paper and, as it happens, I lost the piece of paper when I got up. So what I said came from my toes and it wasn't calculated in that sense.' Kinnock measured the atmosphere of the conference and to the delight of the party activists he made a thundering denunciation of the Conservatives' education cuts. The speech brought the whole conference to life. With constant interruptions for cheering, he accused the Tories of 'pirating scholastic talent from the State sector', 'educational genocide', 'wholesale destruction'. Pouring forth some considerable class venom, he said:

> ... any Party in national government or in local government that perpetuates that kind of crime against ... the standard of living and the opportunities of working-class people and their kids deserves the un-remitting anger of the whole of our society, and we must be at the fist point of that anger in fighting back against the Tories. [Applause] ... they cripple our children and then taunt them for being lame ... our fight for educational advance and progress is not just a fight against the Tories, it is a fight for survival. Let us put all our efforts in every way we can, in our unions, in our work-places, in our Party, everywhere right throughout the whole community into putting education at the top of our priority list. It is the means of progress for our socialism, it is the means of life for our society. [Applause]

Kinnock won a unanimous standing ovation. It was the finest, most momentous and enthusiastically greeted speech of the week, and it changed the mood of the entire conference. For Kinnock it was a crucial moment in his career, and he was now a celebrity. That week he leapt ahead in the NEC elections, getting only 3,000 votes fewer than Tony Benn, who was first in the constituency elections. This was sensational progress: Kinnock was now in second place with 484,000 votes, having increased his vote from fifth place on the NEC in 1978 with 274,000 votes. He benefited from the clean sweep for the left wing in those elections, but the voting clearly showed how popular he now was among the mass of party workers. His increasing popularity within the Party that week was greatly helped by the comedy satire 'End of the Peers Show'. He was the star of the show, and did the linkages for the programme. He greatly enjoyed himself and for months beforehand had been writing jokes on scraps of paper.

Kinnock was now at a most important stage in his career: he was a member of the NEC and the shadow cabinet. Although unheard of other than in South Wales or the Labour Party, he was now standing in the wings of the party leadership. He was not so far to the left as to frighten the centre right of the party and he had superb credentials of service to the left. Moreover, he had not been a member of the government so he bore no responsibility for Labour's general election defeat. Furthermore, as a young rebel he had fought the centre right Labour government on virtually every issue, so there seemed no reason for the left of the Labour Party to suppose that he was not a supporter and a leader of broad left programmes.

At the October 1979 Party conference the Benn-sponsored fringe group, Labour Co-ordinating Committee, blamed Callaghan and Healey for the last government's failure and sought to make the leadership more accountable to the activists through constitutional reform by having the leader elected by the grassroots instead of by MPs; by the reselection of MPs; and the writing of the election manifesto by the NEC. The autumn 1979 conference was a triumph for the left wing over the leadership, on policy making. Although Kinnock had not associated himself with the general brawling over the 'Who runs the Party' dispute at the conference, there seemed no reason to doubt that his sympathies were with the left. The crucial turning-point occurred some months later, when he attacked the left of the Party. Within two years Kinnock would be one of the leading, and one of the most hated, scourges of the far-left wing.

Kinnock's 1979 conference speech was a sign of his popularity among Labour Party workers, but Fleet Street were slow to see just how significant a force he was. He was considered as good entertainment value, not as a future leader. Fleet Street newspapers, as well as the BBC, were mostly too concerned with the demon left-winger, Tony Benn, to take much notice of Kinnock, whose good personal relations with the media enabled him to avoid adverse press comment. The *Guardian* even produced a theory that the Labour Party could only run one horror story at a time, and when Benn was off duty the current ogre was Eric Heffer. Few commentators were thus prepared to take the rising star seriously. It was the popular tabloid newspaper, the *Daily Mirror*, that in June 1979 first reported Kinnock, with considerable scepticism, as a possible future leader. To make his year, on 18 December Kinnock was introduced on the television panel show *Question Time* as a future leader of the Labour Party. Several newspapers, at the New Year, published articles discussing the possibility that Callaghan might resign during 1980. The *Observer* stated that Kinnock could be a possible contender for the leadership, but it was still too early for him. The *News of the World* claimed that he had a good chance of leading the Labour Party, but 1980 would not be Kinnock's year; it was hard to take a court jester seriously, and it advised him to stop acting the fool. General comment in the press at that time was that if Kinnock calmed down he would have a great future in the Labour Party.

Long profiles of Kinnock were published in *The Times* and the *Observer* colour supplement, as the bright young MP. In several interviews with newspapers he said it would be absurd to be in politics and not be ambitious, but he denied that his success had been because of ambition, or calculation:

> At various times in the next 20 or 30 years I think it is reasonable to anticipate that I will be among the leadership of the Labour Party, but as for being leader, I can't see it happening ... I never had any kind of personal ambition and whatever position I have reached now has come without grabbing for it, and I am prepared to continue like that.

In October 1979 Kinnock had denied to Labour left-wingers that, now he was shadow minister, he would knuckle down to the conformity of the leadership, insisting that only the previous week he had spoken at the Party conference in favour of major constitutional alterations in the Labour Party. He proved his point by ignoring the opposition line of abstention in January 1980 when he voted against Government plans to modernize Britain's nuclear weapons system. He was then warned by Callaghan that unless he kept in line, he would be sacked.

It is not known what the effect of the comments that Kinnock should stop being the court jester were, but by June 1980 he had noticeably started to calm down. Those who knew him believe that it was then that his character began to show more depth. When he attended a demonstration against government cuts in arts and education that June, at a Drury Lane theatre, which took the form of songs and sketches by trade union leaders such as Clive Jenkins and Len Murray, he did not join in but limited himself to a simple policy tirade against the Conservatives.

During his parliamentary career Kinnock had often shown the necessary signs of pragmatism essential for successful Labour leaders. Hattersley had, by implication, accused Kinnock of lack of economic realism in the December 1977 party political broadcast. However, in another little-known episode, only weeks later, Kinnock, although considered a left-winger, had defended a report of a Commons select committee on the steel industry, of which he was a member, that had said there would have to be more unemployment in the industry. His father had been a steelworker, and Kinnock had many steelworking families in his constituency. However, he showed great pragmatism in criticizing Labour MPs who, in the hope of instant popularity, created the illusion that the steel industry could survive with no further redundancies. The first signs of this quality of pragmatism, in terms of national policy, were to do with cuts in educational services. This was also the occasion of Kinnock's first split with the far left. At a meeting of the Parliamentary Labour Party, on 8 February, Kinnock met with hostility when he declined to give a commitment to restore the cuts the Conservatives had made in school milk, meals, and travel. Several fellow left-wingers took offence at his slowness to agree that Labour would restore the education cuts, and his insistence that no firm pledges could be given because of uncertainty over Britain's economic prospects. He was accused of 'doing the dirty work' of the Party leadership, and of having succumbed to ambition. Kinnock argued that the future economic circumstances facing a new Labour government might be so severe that it would be impossible to restore the cuts immediately. He said that to promise in advance to do so would be 'hopelessly dishonest', and he would fight to prevent a status quo idea becoming Party policy. In early March, Kinnock attempted to halt the status quo ante policy on the NEC with the help of Michael Foot and Shirley Williams, but was defeated by 14 votes to 3. Several times during the spring he threatened to resign if a pledge in the Party's draft manifesto to restore the Tory cuts in school milk, meals, and travel was approved. He said; 'I disagree with the draft. If it's a choice between making these promises and quitting my front-bench job, frankly the job will have to go.' He claimed it was utterly wrong for Labour to commit itself to such a spending plan. Even if the pledge was approved at the October Party conference, he believed that he might fight on to get it altered. He calculated that, with price increases, Labour could be committing itself to as much as an additional £800 million per year.

The pledge to restore the cuts was approved by the Party conference and was clearly stated in Labour's 1983 general election manifesto. Kinnock quietly forgot about his threat to resign and abided by the conference vote. (On 6 June 1983 he even stated in a televised party political broadcast that if Labour was elected the economies would be restored.) The far-left newspaper *Socialist Worker* published an article in December 1980, viciously denouncing him for his attempt to stop Labour's commitment to restore the cuts. However, as far as the Labour activists were able to see, Kinnock was still committed to the traditional left. He was against capitalism, private medicine, the EEC, the IMF, and nuclear weapons. He was in favour of Clause Four, and public ownership; and his villains were the traditional enemies of the left, the civil service, defence establishment, the Bank of England, and the business community. At the 1980 Party conference he won a standing ovation with his education speech in which he demanded the abolition of public schools, and made bitter personal attacks on the Conservative education ministers, 'Do not let us just get rid of Carlisle and Boyson. Let us declare war on the system that breeds their attitude.' His earlier hedging on the matter of education cuts had been largely forgotten and he was now immensely popular among the party workers. That year in the NEC elections Kinnock was, after Tony Benn, the most popular candidate in the constituency section. However, because of the Labour civil war and the election of Michael Foot as leader, Kinnock's position within the Party was to shift violently.

The modern origin of the advance of the left in the Labour Party stems from the Wilson Government's failure to produce the economic growth promised. Wilson's defeat in 1970 had damaged his prestige as a vote-winner and, within the Party, opposition that was centred around the Tribune Group began to grow against the leadership style of moderate 'gradualism'. A small group known as the Campaign for Labour Party Democracy (CLPD) was established in 1973 with the idea of forcing the Parliamentary Labour Party to accept the decisions of Conference and the NEC. Kinnock had been an early member of this group, but while he agreed that MPs should be selected on a wider Labour Party franchise he was opposed to the idea of compulsory reselection from a short list of more than one. The CLPD had widespread support in the Labour Party because it confined itself strictly to achieving democracy on a wider scale. Its ideological counterpart was the Labour Co-ordinating Committee (LCC), a policy group that supported Tony Benn. Meanwhile, the ranks of the Labour activists had been rapidly joined by pseudo-intellectual and disreputable products of modern polytechnocracy – the very Labourites Kinnock disliked, those to whom socialism was an intellectual stimulus, not a moral crusade.

This New Left had growing and widespread support among a broad section of the Party, who believed that Wilson and Callaghan had wasted Labour's opportunity in government. To them Wilson and later Callaghan, who had been the greatest Labour successes of the past thirty years, were the Judases and quislings of the Party. Bevan, the rebel and a failure who had got nowhere, was a hero. The New Left, who blamed Callaghan and Healey for Labour's 1979 defeat, believed there had been a 'winter of discontent' simply because the Government had ignored Conference and TUC Congress decisions. The LCC thus sought constitutional reform of the Party in order to make the leadership more directly responsible to the activists. The campaign of the left was much better organized, and developed much more quickly than in the 1950s, when Bevan had been pedestalled as it leader. The changing mood within the Party was evident at the 1979 conference. Many of the centre right were shocked at the hatred shown to MPs, whose enclosure took on the appearance of the dock at Nuremberg. With many MPs cowering under such pressure, Conference agreed that the NEC should control the election manifesto, and that there should be compulsory reselection of MPs. The 1980 conference went further, endorsed the reselection of MPs, and agreed to elect the Party leader on a wider franchise, the details of which were to be agreed at a special conference at Wembley in January 1981.

A consequence of this drift was increasing belligerency from a small group of MPs from the right of the Party. In November 1979 the former deputy leader, Roy Jenkins, presented his famous BBC lecture advocating the formation of a new centre party in British politics. Meanwhile other disenchanted personalities, Rogers,

Williams, and Owen, stated that they would leave the Labour Party if it adopted a policy of withdrawal from the Common Market. It is generally not realized that while the right wing were still fighting within the Party, an attempt was made to have Kinnock defeated by the right in his own constituency. In June 1980 an arch-moderate group led by Dr Stephen Haseler, known as the Social Democratic Alliance, a prototype of the SDP, drew up a hit list of fifteen Labour MPs. In addition to Kinnock, other prominent left-wingers on the list were Judith Hart, Eric Heffer, Dennis Skinner, and Joan Lestor. The idea was for the Social Democratic Alliance to field candidates to fight these official Labour MPs at a general election. As Haseler's party later became part of the SDP, the threat never materialized, but it clearly showed that Kinnock, at the time, was still considered by many to be a dangerous left-winger, while when he was elected leader only three years later, he was seen as one of the keenest critics of the far left.

Shortly after the end of the 1980 Party conference, Callaghan resigned the Party leadership, and a new election took place by the old method of MPs' votes only. As the Parliamentary Labour Party had historically, and by the force of necessity, been to the right of the Party as a whole, it was assumed that the leading centre-right candidate, Denis Healey, would be almost certain to be the new Party leader. Healey was also the sensible choice as he was clearly the most popular Labour politician in the country. During the summer, anticipating Callaghan's resignation, Kinnock had, with the help of other Labour MPs, begun canvassing the Parliamentary Labour Party; he found that if Michael Foot were to stand for the leadership he would get as many as 135 votes, precisely the number he would need to win. Kinnock did not think of standing for the leadership himself in 1980, but he wanted to see fielded a 'Stop Healey' candidate. As with the devolution campaign, this leadership contest said much for Kinnock's foresight, energy, guts and determination, in the face of impossible odds, that he was willing to challenge what seemed to be the likelihood of a Healey win. In addition, Kinnock was enthusiastic to see his great friend and adopted father, Michael Foot, elected leader.

Foot's conviction was that somehow the Labour Party had to be held together. However, as a humble and self-effacing man, he was reluctant to stand for the leadership, thinking that his age was against him. He was sixty-seven and would be seventy by the time of another general election. A lifelong Labour rebel, Foot had never sought the leadership; his friends had persuaded him to take almost every senior job he had done in Government. This was a feature that would not have been lost for noting by Kinnock, who, for most of his parliamentary career, has often obscured his own political ambitions by claiming that every step in his career has been by invitation, not from choice; he was, he claims, invited to stand for the District Council, NEC, and the leadership of the Labour Party.

Kinnock and Clive Jenkins, head of the white-collar union ASTMS, decided that the main obstacle to Foot's election was Foot's own reluctance to stand, and arranged for messages to be sent to him urging him to contest the election. It was alleged at the time that it was Foot's wife, Jill Craigie, who had persuaded her husband to stand for election, but the story was quite unfounded. Foot had himself favoured a younger candidate, Peter Shore. But Shore's campaign had been so slow that Foot doubted if he would be able to stop Healey and thus, nominated by Kinnock and Heffer, unwillingly decided to put his own name forward.

The Foot campaign, a desperate attempt to stop Healey, was led by Kinnock who, as Foot's lieutenant, got the campaign team busy lobbying MPs, greatly helped by his, by now large, network of contacts in the constituencies. Moderate Labour MPs, alarmed at local militants, were given to understand that if Foot was elected leader he would visit their constituencies and speak on their behalf. Foot himself was very little help to the campaign, giving the impression that he could not care less. His chances, however, were greatly helped by a book of his that was being serialized at the time by the *Observer*, and a brilliant parliamentary speech he made consisting of aggressive comments against Conservative ministers.

In the first batch of votes on 4 November, Healey was in the lead with 112, Foot had 86, Silkin 38, and Shore 32. Under the election rules Silkin and Shore were both eliminated, having insufficient votes between them to total Foot's. Most of Silkin's votes and many of Shore's then passed to Foot. However, national opinion polls were showing even then that, apart from Tony Benn,

Foot was the most unpopular leader Labour could possibly have. An NOP survey in the *Observer* showed that 75% of the electorate were for Healey, but only 19% for Foot. Voters even preferred Healey to Mrs Thatcher by 45–39%. Nevertheless, the word from the Labour constituency parties was that Foot was by far the most popular choice of leader. MPs, having again been cowed at a party conference a few weeks earlier, worried about reselection, and perhaps believing that Foot would only be a caretaker leader, decided to vote for the old veteran dissenter. Kinnock and the campaign team were now supremely confident that Foot would win. In the final count on 10 November the votes cast were: Healey 129, Foot 139. Kinnock shouted with delight and slammed his fist on the House of Commons Grand Committee table when the voting was announced. In his speech, Foot quoted Bevan's words 'Never underestimate the passion for unity in the Party'.

From the start, Foot's leadership was a great disappointment. The beleaguered MPs' choice of Foot was an Indian summer madness that was to cost Labour dear. Crucial to Foot's election was his immense personal popularity in Parliament; while the composition of the Parliamentary Labour Party itself was swinging to the left, what had impressed those MPs of the centre of the Party who had voted for Foot had been his loyalty to Callaghan, when deputy-leader Foot had indeed urged Callaghan to keep on with the leadership. This lesson of tenacious loyalty to the leadership would also not have been wasted on Kinnock, whose popularity in 1983 among MPs had much to do with his record of consistent defence of Foot. For him Foot's election was an adventure, a splendid opportunity to see the disciple of his hero, Bevan, elected Party leader. Undoubtedly, he could also see that the leadership of the elderly left-winger would sufficiently alter the Party to prepare for his own eventual bid for the leadership. But at this time Kinnock had no clear idea that he might have to make this bid at such an early stage in his career. However, what he did know was that a party that could not win elections was nothing. In this sense, as far as Labour was concerned, his campaigning for Foot was the greatest error made by his heart ruling his head.

Personally and politically, Foot's election as Labour leader was of great significance to Kinnock. Although forever loyal to the

Labour Party, he had spent the ten years of his parliamentary career arguing with the leadership. He had seen the establishment of several of the Party reforms that he favoured, and the election to the leadership of Foot, his old Bevanite hero. Another important development for Kinnock's career was that he was now being taken seriously by his parliamentary colleagues. In the Parliamentary Labour Party elections in December he was elected for the first time to the shadow cabinet: previously he had merely been appointed by Callaghan on Foot's recommendation. Kinnock's 90 votes had just defeated Benn, who only got 88 votes, for a place, and it took two recounts to settle the issue. It was then rumoured that Kinnock had been offered by Foot a more senior portfolio than education, but had refused. His election was the only left-wing success. It was argued by *The Times* that Labour MPs, having been adventurous in electing Michael Foot, decided on caution with the shadow cabinet: Kinnock being considered by the moderates in the PLP to be of the left, but not dangerously so.

On 24 January the special Labour Party conference to consider the wider franchise for the future leadership election met at Wembley. Kinnock, like many of the left, believed that alterations in the Party's constitution were necessary. He thought that constitutional change was a means of survival for the Party. His belief was that the original constitution had been born at a time when socialists were still striving for trade union rights, and against great poverty and injustice; this battle had given the Labour Party a momentum for the first fifty years, but now, he believed, that impetus had been lost. 'Unless we get the participation of a wider and wider section of the people', Labour would be finished. Unlike Foot, he realized that 'You can't live on the memories of the twenties, thirties, and forties'. Various systems of electing a leader had been considered. Roy Hattersley at the time had the idea of giving every member of the Labour Party one vote. This had been turned down by the left-wing NEC which had advocated a system of groups of votes. The formula favoured by the Parliamentary Labour Party, Foot, Kinnock, and the moderate trade unions, was that 50% of the votes would come from the PLP, 25% from the constituencies, and 25% from the unions. The NEC had opted for 33.3% to each. At the conference the bitter atmosphere shocked many traditional Labour voters, even Sir Harold Wilson was moved to describe the new young Labour activists as 'fascists'. Despite the confidence of the moderates that the 50-25-25 scheme would be passed, the left moved quickly to get their motion for 30% from the constituencies, 40% from the trade unions and 30% from the PLP accepted. (Arguably, had the 30-40-30 system been in operation when Attlee quit the leadership in 1955, Bevan would have won easily.) Foot had been against this scheme of giving 40% of the votes to the trade unions and 30% to the constituencies that was eventually accepted; but had done nothing. It had been a major test of his leadership and he had failed.

Later that week the 'Gang of Four', Owen, Rogers, Williams, and Jenkins, met and issued the 'Limehouse Declaration', thus forming the Social Democratic Party (SDP). With considerable media sympathy, the SDP advertised for public support and immediately obtained a sizeable membership and generous financial contributions. Opinion polls in March showed the SDP already securing 30% of the popular vote, a figure surpassing that of the other main parties. Hitherto there had been no attacks on the SDP by the Labour leadership. Kinnock, however, who had a tenacious loyalty to the Labour Party, had little affection for middle-class socialists of the likes of the SDP, and was infuriated. Initially he was slow to calculate the damage that the SDP might do to Labour, believing that the Party could spare a few 'shavings' from the moderate wing. Already in January he had told the Social Democrats that they should decide whether they wanted to leave the Party. As Labour prepared to defend a majority of 10,000 at the Warrington by-election, Kinnock virtually single-handedly launched the Party's attack against the SDP. In a fiery speech that won him a standing ovation at the Welsh Labour Party conference in June, he denounced the Social Democrats as 'traitors'. He said the SDP was a party invented by television: 'They couldn't get a more favourable or sycophantic media treatment if they had won the World Cup in the year of the marriage of Prince Charles.' Labour's fortunes sank even lower in July when Roy Jenkins took 42.4% of the vote at Warrington.

Labour was now in a pitiful state. Financially impoverished, and with a frail leader, it was fighting on three fronts; against the

Conservative Party, the militant left, and the Social Democrats. As the 30% PLP, 40% trade union and 30% constituency party voting system had been established, Benn announced his intention of contesting the job of deputy leader. Kinnock was furious at the quarrel that was wrecking the Labour Party, but it was Benn's decision to challenge Healey for the deputy leadership that threw him into despair. From this time on he did not think that Labour would win the 1983 general election. Benn was practically isolated among senior Labour leaders in his campaign for the deputy leadership, most of whom, from Foot downwards, anticipated five months of bitter and totally unnecessary division. Kinnock was one of the last to attack Benn and made a widely reported speech on 25 April 1981 in Lincolnshire. His speech was significant because only he could match Benn's popularity among the constituency activists which provided most of Benn's votes at Party conferences. Like other leading Labour politicians, Kinnock did not name Benn in his speech but it was widely interpreted as referring to him and his supporters. He said:

> If they think that unity can be won or support gained by giving the impression that major policies can be simultaneously fulfilled in a few weeks of government they are offering a fantasy that insults adult intelligence, invites derision and guarantees disappointment ... mutual distrust on the scale that has developed between some parts of the party has been damaging, is wounding and if it continues, will be lethal .... The arrogant, the obsessive, those whose political activity consists of attacking or defending the past, those who give their energies to inventing a fictitious future, must recognize that. Otherwise they must leave now to become the insignificant ravers in the unimportant fragments that they would be without the status and opportunity the Labour Party gives them.

The madness of the deputy leadership contest was shown when Labour lost elections at Croydon North West and then at Crosby to the SDP grouping. Even though Benn had to go to hospital for treatment of a rare nervous disease, the bitter dispute continued. Kinnock denied that he personally disliked Benn: however, this seems unlikely, as Benn, who was Viscount Stansgate until he renounced his title, personified the middle-class socialism that Kinnock mistrusted. Hitherto Kinnock had attacked Benn for standing, but had not opposed his campaign: now his mind was changed by a speech made in June by the Yorkshire miners' leader, Arthur Scargill, who had said that those 'who openly criticized Tony Benn and, by implication, supported the candidature of Denis Healey', were 'sabotaging not only the candidature of Tony Benn but the principles of socialism which are basic to our movement'. Kinnock deplored these tactics of guilt by association, and the slandering of Benn's critics as being 'careerist'. Worse still was the fact that Benn made no effort to dissociate himself from these attacks.

To be certain of winning, Benn had to count on getting the votes of eighty-seven MPs: he was confident that this could be achieved as it was thought the ninety-strong Tribune Group would support him. There was, however, a disorganized faction of some twenty to thirty Tribune MPs, including Kinnock, who believed that Benn's election as deputy leader would do the Party much harm. Within this group there were various unco-ordinated moves to stop Benn, such as a letter, signed by twenty Labour MPs, advocating that Party members should vote for Silkin in the first round, and abstain in the second. Although this group did not have a leader, Kinnock, as the parliamentarian most willing to speak to the press, was the group's senior media voice and was thus considered the head of the crucial Tribunite 'Stop Benn' movement. On 15 September Kinnock's Bedwellty constituency Labour Party voted heavily, 53 to 11, to support Tony Benn's candidature. Kinnock, however, informed his constituency that he would not abide by their decision and would be voting for Silkin as deputy leader. He told the meeting that he had made his decision 'on the basis of making a very strong appeal for people who realize that the real enemies of the Labour Party are the Conservatives and now indeed the Social Democrats, and we fight them better as a united force'. That week Kinnock appeared on the BBC *Newsnight* programme and said that the attitudes that equated loyalty to Benn with loyalty to the Labour movement were a dangerous threat to the values of democratic socialism. On the 17th another popular constituency-section member of the NEC, Joan Lestor, also stated that she intended to defy her local party and vote for Silkin. She said that those who were implying retribution against those who failed to support Tony

Benn were showing that it was an election of personality, because there was little policy difference between Benn and Silkin.

To most Labour activists a vote for Benn was an absolute loyalty test for those who claimed to be left-wingers. Kinnock had a long history of loyalty to left-wing causes: even on the matter of school meal increases he had eventually agreed to the party line. His friends, such as Barbara Castle, believed that although he clearly had convictions, he was too gregarious and too much of a joker ever to make himself unpopular in the party. Thus many of his friends were surprised, and some shocked, when he began his campaign to stop Benn. On 18 September the national press leaked details of Kinnock's famous and carefully written 3,000-word article, published in *Tribune*.

In this article, entitled 'Personality, Policies and Democratic Socialism', written with no prompting from Foot, Kinnock stated that he had nominated Silkin for deputy leader, and gave his reasons why he would not be voting for either Benn or Healey. He said that while he enjoyed friendly relations with Denis Healey, there were issues of policy, and notably unilateral disarmament, that made it impossible to endorse him in a contest for office. Kinnock said that his arguments for not voting for Benn had relatively little to do with policies and much more to do with presentation of policies and the difficulties of their implementation in government. He argued that the Labour Party was in a seriously weak political position that had been made immeasurably worse by the nature and the conduct of the deputy leadership election campaign. He furiously, and prophetically, warned that if Labour had more years of distraction, it would defeat itself at another general election. 'Those who scorn appeals for unity . . . desert the millions of people for whom a Labour Government would be the only means of deliverance from insecurity, poverty, unemployment and despair.' He believed that by the time of a general election in 1983, the spending resources available to the Conservative government for vote-buying, reflation, the reorganization of parliamentary boundaries, and the presence of the SDP as a non-Conservative alternative, could combine to deny Labour democratic power. Kinnock criticized a speech that Benn had made to an ASLEF conference during which Benn had insisted that the Party should have a proper democratic structure that would make sure the Parliamentary Labour Party adhered to policies agreed at Conference. The logic of Benn's argument and that of the militant left, Kinnock said, was that Labour MPs who did not abide by Conference decisions should fail to be reselected by their constituency parties. He believed that 'democratic structures' were a sensible adjustment in the development of an eighty-year-old party, but the changes should not be in terms of threats of MPs being dismissed but of changes in the conditions of work. Kinnock argued that no worthy Labour MP could adhere to dog-licence arguments. He then went on to argue that Benn had given 'false hopes to those who believe that monumental changes can be wrought by the device of reforming the party constitution'. He concluded:

> I believe that Tony has fostered antagonism within the party, he has undermined the credibility of credible policies by over-simplification, he has not disowned those who insist upon support for his candidature as the test of loyalty to Labour policy. I believe that, through an inaccurate analysis of the position and power of the Labour movement and by a tactically mistaken decision to contest the deputy leadership in 1981, Tony has significantly harmed the current standing and electoral opportunities of the Labour Party. By so doing he has inadvertently harmed those who I am sure he most wants to help.

The elections for the deputy leadership were held at Brighton, during the September Labour Party conference. The event had been billed by Fleet Street as a landmark in the history of the Labour Party. In the glare of the television lights the Party general secretary announced the percentages of votes cast: Silkin 18, Benn 36, Healey 45. Silkin was now eliminated. In the final count, in which 16 Tribunite MPs, lead by Kinnock, abstained, the final percentage count was Benn 49.574%, and Healey 50.426%. Kinnock had fought against Benn because he believed Benn, as deputy leader, would be disastrous for the Party.

However much damage he thought a Benn deputy leadership might do, Kinnock himself was keenly ambitious with a strong instinct for the preservation of his own political life. So after the first count for the deputy leadership, when he was certain that Benn was going to win, he went to a gathering of journalists in the lobby of the Metropole Hotel and told them he thought Benn was going to win, adding that he had nothing against Benn personally and was prepared to work with him. A short while later, when Healey won the contest, Kinnock went about Brighton telling journalists that what he had said earlier was, of course, not for publication.

It was the abstention by Kinnock and his fellow MPs which spared the Labour Party from Benn's deputy leadership. Indeed, Kinnock was now the unwilling hero of the moderates and was headlined in the *Observer* as 'The Man Who Saved the Labour Party'. However, to the party activists and many of the left, he was suddenly a heretic and a traitor who had wrecked Benn's campaign. The previous year, Kinnock had been heralded at the Party conference as the left's great discovery – now he was hissed and taunted as a 'socialist Judas'. To make matters worse, he proceeded to vote against the proposal that the party election manifesto should be written by the NEC, a move which only the previous year he had supported. He also helped Judith Hart and Joan Lestor defeat a Bennite motion demanding that PLP votes should be noted. Speaking at the Tribune meeting, Kinnock was badly heckled, but said, 'It's been a hell of a year, this past week. And I don't offer an apology, I claim the right to speak.' Kinnock was badly shaken by the hatred that he encountered, and was involved in numerous arguments. He was attacked by a Bennite supporter, who kicked him so badly on the arm that he had trouble writing for months. Kinnock approached his assailant and beat him severely.

Having successfully defended Michael Foot's leadership from the threat of Tony Benn, Kinnock had to return home to account for his actions. At a meeting organized by the University of Cardiff Labour Club, he was heckled and fiercely criticized for wrecking the career of the folk hero of the left, Tony Benn. Speakers at the meeting were incredulous that Kinnock could let Healey, who was opposed to the main policies of Conference, such as withdrawal from the Common Market and unilateral nuclear disarmament, win the deputy leadership. Kinnock then encountered a furious general management committee at his South Wales constituency. During 1981, because of his increasing recognition of the need for pragmatic politics and his support for the leadership, as personified by Michael Foot, he had found himself more and more at odds with his constituency party. He had anticipated trouble at the meeting that week, but hoped to persuade his critics by argument. He dismissed the possibility of his failure to do so with a shrug of the shoulders, believing that 'if the price of popularity is the auction of your integrity, it's not worth a damn'. But he was already finding the personal attacks on him emotionally most hurtful, and at the Friday constituency meeting, after savage attacks from the floor against him, some of his loyalist supporters were so upset that they left the meeting.

To an increasingly radical section in the constituency, as well as the far left of the Labour Party in the country as a whole, Kinnock's defiance of his local party's wishes was an act of war. Only the previous year he had been considered such a firmly committed left-winger that there had been an attempt by the Labour right-wingers to oust him from his constituency. Now he had to endure the agonizing trauma of MP reselection, a system which he himself had fought so hard to see Labour adopt for every constituency in the country. However, his personal popularity was such that his opponent, Davies, a local steelworker and left-winger, although he had won the support of several of the constituency wards, never stood a chance. At the Bedwellty constituency party reselection meeting, in March, the general management committee voted to continue with Kinnock as their parliamentary candidate; 12 votes to Davies and 62 to Kinnock. Kinnock thanked the meeting for a magnificent five to one vote of confidence, adding 'Now for the battle to defeat the Tories and implement socialism'.

But the far left of the Labour Party were unforgiving, and an orchestrated attempt was planned to remove Kinnock and Joan Lestor from the NEC. In early 1982 a far-left-wing group known as 'Labour Liaison '82' was formed and conducted a series of meetings which were arranged by the Bennite journal *London Labour Briefing*, and poorly attended by some seventy left-wingers, at the Greater London Council offices in County Hall. The original purpose of the meetings was to ensure that Conference decisions were incorporated in future election manifestos; to make certain that this was done it was decided that there should be a suitable and appropriate 'slate' of left-wing candidates for the NEC elections.

However, it was soon clear that the real purpose of the meetings was to vote Kinnock and Lestor off the NEC and replace them with Norman Atkinson and Audrey Wise. Prominent in this movement were Tony Benn and Chris Mullin, editor of *Tribune*. Later on, during the 1983 leadership election campaign, when it was clear that Kinnock was going to be the new Labour leader, the ambitious Chris Mullin denied any knowledge of this attempt to throw Kinnock off the NEC.

Kinnock believed his defence of Foot's leadership was more important than his own place on the NEC: if he lost his place it was just unfortunate. He was, however, concerned at the attacks on his own personal credibility and fearful for the damage that the argument was doing to the Labour Party.

At a Tribune Group meeting at Westminster, in the spring, Reg Race, a Bennite Labour MP, said that Joan Lestor and Kinnock, because he had wavered concerning restoring education cuts, could no longer be classed as left wing, and should be removed from the Tribune 'slate' of seven candidates for the NEC elections due to be held at the autumn Party conference. Robin Cook, Labour MP for Edinburgh Central, who was later to be Kinnock's campaign manager in the 1983 leadership election, spoke against this, claiming it would plunge the Party into further dispute. Kinnock's response was immediately to send a letter to Race, which he released to the press, challenging him to produce evidence of his spending cuts allegations. At a vicious Tribune Group meeting on 14 June the attempt to form a Tribune 'slate' collapsed. Cook argued for a scheme that would endorse the present constituency section of the NEC, including Lestor and Kinnock. That was displaced by a compromise resolution that merely stated it was the prerogative of the constituency parties to vote for whom they wanted, while deploring personal attacks on members of the NEC. The compromise resolution was eventually passed and Lestor and Kinnock were thus not to be protected by a seven-candidate slate when fighting for their NEC seats in the autumn. Kinnock's place on the NEC survived the autumn conference election vote, but his popularity among the constituencies temporarily declined.

For Kinnock, having been the great architect of Foot's election as leader, the main concern after autumn 1980 had been to fight as

Foot's defender. By the time of the November 1981 Crosby by-election, Labour's opinion-poll standing was the lowest for thirty-five years. Foot's indecisiveness and pitiful lack of the qualities of leadership made it appear that government was not for him. However, Foot himself could not be blamed; he had not sought the leadership, but had been unwisely persuaded by his friends. A decent, kind hearted and most honourable man, Foot was unreasonably blamed for Labour's troubles. However, what was not generally appreciated was that Foot was unfortunate enough to be leader during an extremely difficult time in Labour's history and he was not given due credit for his determined efforts to hold the Party together. Labour MPs were already concerned at Foot's lack of energy and concentration, and that week a crisis meeting was held at the House of Commons to discuss his leadership. Moderate MPs were angry at his permitting Benn and Heffer to retain the chairmanships of important NEC committees; Kinnock had also pleaded with him to sack Benn from the influential NEC Home Policy Committee. However, Foot, in the interests of keeping a balanced team, insisted that Benn should be kept on. Suddenly, with no consultation with the shadow cabinet, Benn made a parliamentary speech pledging Labour to the compulsory purchase of North Sea oil. Kinnock was furious at the damage Benn was doing to Labour's public image and said: 'Do you realize that you are the only one who can save us and win the general election?' Later, when speculation increased that Benn was again hoping to fight Healey for the deputy leadership, Kinnock said he believed it could prove 'terminal' for the Labour Party. Foot now agreed with Kinnock to deal with Benn, and ordered MPs not to vote for him in the shadow cabinet elections. However, such was his lack of authority that he was defied by sixty-seven MPs who insisted on voting for the unsuccessful Benn.

Kinnock's attemps to make Foot take action against Benn had won him much sympathy among moderate Labour MPs, and his popularity was such that he achieved seventh place in the November 1981 shadow cabinet elections. However, his turning away from the far left was criticized by *Tribune* as being careerist, for he was now attacking the very Party members who had helped him with his promotion. He was not however so disliked by the left as to be taken off the Tribune Group 'slate' for the shadow cabinet elections, and there was even speculation that he would be promoted from the education portfolio. That winter, as the party moderates began to fight against the left, Foot, supported by Kinnock, led the voting on the NEC by 10 votes to 9 to establish an enquiry into the activities of the Militant Tendency and rejected the application of Tariq Ali to join the Labour Party. Kinnock, by voting for Foot, had not only appeared to have saved the latter's leadership but, to a large section of Benn's supporters, his had been the deciding voice that had prevented the far left from winning a bitterly fought campaign.

However, the Conservatives were doing no better, for opinion polls suggested that Mrs Thatcher was the most unpopular Prime Minister in living memory; it therefore seemed unthinkable, unless there was a dramatically noticeable improvement in performance, that her Government could win another term of office. The major parties were equally unpopular, each obtaining only 30% of the opinion poll vote, until April 1982, when the Falklands War occurred that was to decisively alter the fortunes of the Conservative Party.

Britain had decolonized most of her last remaining dependent territories during the 1960s, when Callaghan and Healey had been senior ministers. Both knew the dangerous consequences that could follow if the Falklands guard-ship HMS *Endurance* was withdrawn. Callaghan, when Prime Minister, had taken a great interest in the dependent territories and, a not generally known fact, in 1979 he improved the defences of the newly independent nations and British colonies in the Caribbean. But there were no ministers in the Thatcher Government from the great era of decolonization and none had knowledge of colonial defence. As a consequence of the 1981 Defence White Paper of Defence Secretary and former merchant banker John Nott, the Conservative Government decided to withdraw HMS *Endurance*. Callaghan pleaded with Mrs Thatcher not to do this. Speaking in the House of Commons on 9 February 1982 he had said: 'I beg you, Prime Minister, not to scrap the *Endurance*.' She ignored this advice from the most knowledgeable parliamentary authority on colonial matters, stating, 'It was a difficult decision for the Defence Minister to make but I realize his reasons for doing so.' The *Endurance* was withdrawn and in April the Falklands were invaded. The words of the nineteenth-century Lord Cardwell had long been forgotten: 'Let it be known that war with a colony is war with England.'

Kinnock agreed with the sending of the task force, and believed this was 'necessary and unavoidable'. However, his greatest concern at this time was to defend Foot's leadership. Foot began well by making one of the finest speeches of his career in the House of Commons at the time of the invasion but he refused to co-operate with inter-party discussions and seemed to lack energy for the fight. Many commentators were misled into believing that he was not really a staunch patriot because he supported CND; certainly Labour did not support the Government with any great enthusiasm although they did approve of the British use of military force. Foot was attacked within his own party by some for supporting the Government's invasion of the Falklands and the dissenting voice of Judith Hart, widely reported by the media, did Labour's credibility much harm. Kinnock saw the danger for Labour of not being in tune with the public over the Falklands issue and wrote an article for *Tribune* defending Foot's support of the Government during a time of national crisis; he rightly feared that the war might increase its popularity.

After the Falklands War was over a committee of inquiry was set up under the chairmanship of Lord Franks; rather as in *Murder on the Orient Express* the committee could find no one guilty because everyone was to blame. In December 1941 the battleships *Prince of Wales* and *Repulse*, which Churchill had unwittingly sent to the Far East with no proper air cover, had been sunk with great loss of life. Churchill had then had the magnanimity to admit that he was wrong: 'I didn't know, I wasn't told, I should have asked.' Although Mrs Thatcher and Nott were competent in the administration of the Falklands War, no one in Britain was more responsible for the war taking place. That they were able to enhance their reputations in spite of this is among the most disgraceful injustices of modern British politics.

The 'Falklands Factor' produced a dramatic improvement in the fortunes of the Conservative Party, and by the time of the Argentine surrender on 14 June, it seemed certain that Labour would have no chance of success at a future general election. Kinnock, who was now firmly established among the Labour leadership, brought some life to the campaign for the Mitcham and Morden by-election when he criticized Foreign Secretary Francis Pym, who had hinted that the Conservatives might soon have a general election to capitalize on their Falklands popularity. Kinnock said, 'I really think we have seen the Conservative Party stooping into the very sewer of public emotion if it is contemplating holding an election on the basis of the Falklands crisis, for which they are very largely responsible.' He added that if an election were to take place 'it would be an act of the most profound cynicism on the part of the Conservative Party'.

Kinnock now began to reassess his stance within the Party. In the summer of 1982 he quit the editorial board of *Tribune*. The paper had been useful to him when he was the darling of the left for articles by him were published most weeks which made his name known to Labour Party activists. He had been an unsalaried director on the board for five years, during which time he had been asked to resign several times because of his frequent absence from board meetings. Now he used this as an excuse for quitting. A more likely reason is that he wished to distance himself from the far left and to demonstrate his displeasure with the newly appointed Bennite editor, Chris Mullin. Kinnock drove 250 miles deliberately to cast his vote against him.

In the spring of 1982 Kinnock was in a position to make a powerful bid for the leadership. However, he claims that it was not until early 1983 when trade union leaders 'invited' him to put his name forward that he even considered deliberately contesting the leadership. Despite this denial of ambition, his story seems unlikely. His main work of education policy formulation had practically ceased by the spring of 1982, when his findings were incorporated into 'Labour's Programme', a guidebook to Bennite Britain. As there was not much government education legislation in preparation, and as Kinnock, as chief education spokesman, could only speak at Westminster on the subject of his portfolio, there was not much work for him to do. The pages of *Hansard* show that he made very few Commons speeches in 1982, and it was also noted by parliamentary correspondents that year that Kinnock was seldom ever seen. What he was doing was touring the country assiduously cultivating his contacts with the trade unions. Kinnock denies this, and claims that he was doing no more than his usual hundred mini-tours a year. This is correct, but whereas he had previously mainly visited schools and constituency Labour parties, now he was increasingly accepting invitations to speak at union conferences. Since the new regulations for the leadership election franchise were 30% from the PLP and the constituencies and 40% from the trade unions, he and his advisers knew that he had to increase his popularity among unionists.

Kinnock had campaigned for Labour in a series of disastrous by-elections: he would thus have heard the views of the electorate on the doorsteps and in the constituencies, that Foot should go. He would have heard this on his mini-tours, that made him probably the most travelled person in British public life. He would have seen the evidence of the opinion surveys that showed that if Foot departed from the leadership it would mean an immediate improvement of ten points. His special friendship with Foot would have made him uniquely able to persuade Foot to quit the leadership. But Kinnock did nothing. There was no other MP who had done as much work, and had campaigned as hard, for Labour, no one else who had shown such total dedication to the Party as Kinnock had. Yet despite this dedication, and the knowledge that Labour might not win a general election with Foot as its leader, Kinnock did nothing to persuade Foot to quit. Despite his loyalty to the Labour Party and his determination to see it win, Kinnock's personal loyalty to Foot was greater.

The Thatcher government still had two years of office left, and with a waning 'Falklands Factor' and three million unemployed, Labour could still just win by a miracle, with Foot as its leader. Kinnock was still only forty, and those who knew him at this time claim that he was not yet seriously thinking in terms of the leadership but more in terms of the deputy leadership for he knew that a fresh struggle for the leadership would only cast the Party into more confusion. There was also a genuine fear that a leadership contest would be won by a moderate such as Denis Healey. However much Kinnock wanted Labour to form a new government, he was still firmly of the broad left; he believed in unilateral disarmament and Labour's other disastrous policies, and was passionately determined that the major Party constitutional changes that had been won should not go to waste. Whether or not he would ever become leader of the Party, he did not want the Party of the Wilson era: an indication of Labour's general drift to the left.

At the Blackpool conference in September, Foot's leadership was being further attacked, and there were claims that there were trade union chieftains and senior Labour moderates who were attempting to muster support for a substitute. Kinnock was most vocal in his defence of Michael Foot, insisting that the speculation concerning the leadership had to stop, otherwise it would cripple Labour electorally. He warned that it would be the Labour moderates who would be to blame if Labour was defeated at the general election, if they replaced left-wing arguments concerning policy and constitutional matters with a conspiracy against Foot's leadership. This was a dramatic switch in his defence of this leadership, which he had until then confined to Foot's enemies on the left of the Party. Kinnock's open attack on the moderates of the Parliamentary Labour Party, whose support had previously been vital to him to secure his election to the shadow cabinet, showed his now increasingly powerful position within the Party. However, he saved most of his aggression for the Conservative Party and for the far left.

At the *Tribune* rally Kinnock was booed when he criticized a small group of MPs who had abandoned the Tribune Group to form an organization to campaign with unions and activists. However, this was a conference week when Labour was trying desperately to patch up its disunited image. In the elections for the NEC Joan Lestor suffered for failing to support Benn in the 1981 deputy leadership contest, and was voted off. Kinnock, who had been the chief of the broad left's 'Stop Benn' campaign, was saved by his widespread personal popularity, only dropping to a credible fifth place with 371,000 votes. His popularity was again shown in the standing ovation that he won for his education speech, in which he made a savage class-hatred attack on the Conservatives:

> We have seen in the last three years the children, the young people, the adults of this country who need to use the public education system, subject to unremitting attack from a government which is supposed to have not only moral but legal responsibility for safeguarding the edu-

cational interests of the nation. They have made that attack with a ferocity, on a scale, at a pace that is unequalled anywhere in the civilized world. When Margaret Thatcher said in Chicago in 1978, 'Let some of the children grow taller than others', she was not talking about your kids. That is for certain.... The whole story of that education policy ... has been of stunted provision.

The Party conference had seen the establishment of a centre right majority on the NEC that meant a right-wing purge on the NEC policy committees, and the removal of Benn from the Home Policy chairmanship. Foot had eventually withdrawn his support from Tony Benn, under pressure from Kinnock. There had also been a consolidation of the right in the shadow cabinet, where in this November's elections there were no alterations to the fifteen portfolios. However, Kinnock's new and greatly increased popularity amongst MPs meant that he was now in second place in the shadow cabinet elections, having only been seventh a year earlier. This was sensational progress as he had otherwise never been considered very seriously by Labour MPs. The significance of these votes was that Kinnock, a year before he was elected leader, had already achieved a balanced spread of support from the unions, MPs and constituencies.

Foot now wanted to promote Kinnock to a more senior portfolio that would be in keeping with his importance and value to the Party, and decided to move him from education to the job of shadow Employment Minister that was currently held by Eric Varley. However, Varley lobbied for support among other moderate MPs and was successfully able to stop Foot's attempt to move him. Kinnock's friends claim that it was Varley's humiliation of Foot which persuaded Kinnock to go for the leadership. Foot then told Kinnock that he would conduct a campaign to sack Varley, but Kinnock assured him that such a move would cause the Party great harm, and that he would go for the leadership instead. Kinnock denies this account and claims that a number of other factors made him decide to campaign for the leadership. Whichever is correct, it is clear that by the autumn of 1982, although he had very few duties on the shadow cabinet, Kinnock had given up coaching his mini rugby team, and was campaigning among the trade unions.

The new leadership contest would be fought on the recent 30–40–30 franchise which would favour a candidate who was popular with the party activists such as Tony Benn. But to be leader, Benn would need to be an MP, and alterations in constituency boundaries meant that Benn's constituency in Bristol, where he had been an MP for thirty-two years, had disappeared. As probably the most controversial British politician, he would need to find a constituency with a massively secure Labour majority to have any chance of a seat at Westminster. He was offered other constituencies but claimed that he wished to be loyal to the people of Bristol: he was then selected for the new electorally hopeless constituency of Bristol East.

Kinnock's visits to trade union conferences greatly increased during early 1983. As the unions were now having growing doubts about Foot's ability to win a general election, Kinnock claims that it was in the spring of 1983 that various union chiefs said to him that should the time come when he cared to put himself forward for the leadership, they would be pleased to nominate him. Of critical significance also was the support he won from leading moderate John Golding, who succeeded Tony Benn as chairman of the Home Policy Committee. Kinnock's hard line with the left and Militant had brought him valuable goodwill among the Parliamentary Party and made him acceptable to the Party moderates.

In the East London constituency of Bermondsey the Labour MP Bob Mellish had created a good deal of animosity in the local party by accepting the deputy chairmanship of the London Docklands Development Corporation. Mellish had not made clear his intention to continue as an MP and on the assumption that he would be retiring, his constituency party began to look for a successor and selected a far left candidate, Peter Tatchell. Kinnock was against the selection of Tatchell as a candidate and had voted on the NEC Organization Committee in December 1981 that had opposed Tatchell. Foot was also against him because he had seen an article that Tatchell had published in a far left journal, advocating militant opposition to parliamentary government, so he said in Parliament that Tatchell would not be endorsed as a candidate as long as he, Foot, was leader of the Labour Party. However, by January 1983 Foot had changed his mind and, ignoring Kinnock, voted on the

NEC to endorse Tatchell. Tatchell was then defeated, although Bermondsey had been one of Labour's safest constituencies. Foot's leadership was in a state of crisis. A survey at the time showed that 96 of 117 Labour MPs, who were 'festering with discontent', thought that Foot should go before a June election. However, speaking on a Bermondsey election platform, Kinnock said that he would not persuade Foot to quit the leadership. Foot stated that if people wanted him to go then a candidate should be put up against him to contest the leadership. Were Foot to quit, Healey would automatically be leader until the autumn Party conference when he would have to stand for election; Kinnock, Silkin or Heffer looked like possible deputy leaders. The test of Foot's leadership was to be the Darlington by-election in March 1983; it would be essential for Labour to win this if it were to have any hope of forming a government. When Labour did win Darlington with a slightly increased majority, some of the great concern surrounding Foot's leadership among Labour MPs was eased: no attempts were made to ask him to go because he was held in such great personal affection. Kinnock was the loudest in Foot's defence. Speaking at an Ebbw Vale public meeting on 4 March he said of Foot, 'I want him to be leader of our country, for I trust him with my children's lives. I trust him with the future of our people.' The threat to Foot's leadership also produced defensive action by the EEPTU, COHSE and AEUW unions who were quick to dispel stories that their confidence in Foot was wavering. In February the Tribune Group also demanded that support for Foot should continue. That this movement for Labour unity should be led by Tony Benn, Kinnock considered contemptible.

Meanwhile the Conservatives were delighted that Foot was being kept on as leader. A Marplan survey in March showed the SDP was now the second most popular party. The Conservatives were the most popular with 41%, the SDP polled 31%, and Labour only 27%. With increasing speculation concerning a general election in June, Labour produced an agreement with the trade unions on wage controls, in the form of a national economic assessment. This, however, contributed to Labour's old-fashioned image; it was no longer necessary for the Party to claim that only it could work with the unions, as the years of economic recession had made these a spent force. Labour then produced a much criticized draft election manifesto 'The New Hope for Britain', that was a poorly boiled-down version of 'Labour's Programme'. In Parliament, rumours were rife about a possible general election, and Mrs Thatcher announced that to protect the country from speculation there would be a general election on 9 June 1983.

Slowly over the years, as this chapter has shown, Neil Kinnock had built up wide support within the Labour Party. He was much liked by constituency workers for bothering to speak to them; he was initially admired by the Tribunite left for defying his party's leadership; middle-of-the-road Labour MPs saw him as a moderating influence on the more extreme left and were impressed by his loyalty to Foot; the unions admired him for not forgetting his working-class origins, for his eloquence and pragmatism. He appeared to be an affable, honest, hardworking fighter for the Labour cause.

He had not been a great success as shadow Minister for Education but the portfolio had mellowed him; his travels round the country had made him harshly conscious of the problems each area faced and he had gradually distanced himself from the more extreme elements in the Party and occupied a more central position. He was now poised to make a bid for the leadership.

6 · The 1983 General Election

Despite the weeks of speculation concerning a general election, Mrs Thatcher's announcement had caught Labour by surprise. There were 150 constituencies where Labour candidates had not been selected. More significantly, the Boundary Commission alterations were anticipated to give the Conservatives an instant advantage of an additional twenty-one seats. The Conservatives started the campaign with a massive 47% of support in public opinion surveys, against Labour's 34% and the SDP's 19%. However, Labour believed that, if it could make what it assumed to be the popular discontent concerning the 3 million unemployed the main election issue, it might have a chance of winning by default. However, unemployment had now become a tired issue, and Labour was unable to sustain much interest in the subject, having failed to appreciate that the pragmatic British, despite inadequate dole money, had been able to adapt to the situation. Labour thus began the campaign by being even more unpopular than in 1979, when with only 36.9% it got its lowest share of the vote for fifty years. During the month-long 1983 campaign Labour found that its limited popularity declined still further.

Kinnock had now spent four years as a shadow Education Minister, and was an influential voice within the Party. The 1983 election was his first major trial as a senior Labour politician. He threw himself into his campaigning, touring the country, speaking at more than a hundred constituencies, more than any other member of the Labour leadership. In Scotland he even spoke at seven constituencies in an afternoon. He worked a gruelling itinerary, doing a certain amount of canvassing, but concentrating his energies on public meetings. He spoke everywhere: at pitheads, factory canteens, constituency hustings, often getting only four or five hours' sleep each night. During the early part of the campaign he even had trouble with his voice. He campaigned enthusiastically, like a missionary who could not bear to miss the chance of saving a soul. His tendency to linger after meetings, arguing with those whom he had failed to convince from the platform, was the despair of his organizers. His determination to speak to as many people as possible wrought havoc to his campaign programme, and his reputation for arriving late at meetings did not improve. Among journalists Kinnock's habitual lateness was becoming as legendary as Shirley Williams's. On one occasion arrangements had been made for him to speak to a meeting of a hundred workers at a BL car factory at Erdington. Kinnock arrived late, by which time most of the workers had left and the meeting-place was nearly empty: undeterred, he spoke to the remaining few with his customary verve. His campaigning, and his popularity among the constituency parties, meant that when a survey of Labour candidates was conducted by *The Times*, as to who should succeed Foot as leader, half chose Kinnock. Among the new generation of Labour MPs Kinnock was even more of a favourite than traditional left-wing personalities such as Eric Heffer.

The enthusiasm of Kinnock's campaign meant that he would sometimes be so hypnotized by his own speaking that he would make absurd claims. At a socialist meeting in Northampton he stated that another term of the Conservatives' 'resolute approach' would mean 'a national unemployment rate of at least 25%'. He said there was no prospect of economic improvement as the slump had only slowed down from a collapse to a crumble. 'Anyone voting Conservative is voting for more collapse, insecurity and economic disaster.' His fiery language was what the party faithful wanted to hear, but it was hardly likely to be taken seriously by the wavering voters, which was essential if Labour was to win. Oblivious to this he continued his scaremongering, telling a Cardiff audience that it was not that the Conservative government could not do anything to lift the country out of the slump, but that it would not. 'No one should fool themselves that if she wins, Margaret Thatcher will change direction. If she wins, the people of Britain will have volunteered for the slump society.'

During the election campaign, Kinnock missed few opportunities to speak to his growing contacts in the trade unions. On 23 May, while doing a tour of the North West, he spoke at the UCW conference, at Douglas, Isle of Man. Foot was originally to have spoken, but when the general election was ordered, his office notified the UCW that he would not be able to attend. The UCW then asked Kinnock, and arranged transport in a light aircraft to enable him to resume his campaign programme in the afternoon. He said the Conservatives were fighting a war with the trade unionists. 'The battlefield is littered with the ruins of industries, of communities, of services and peoples' lives.' Britain, he said, was governed by a secret police force known as unemployment, and the fear which it caused. Thatcherism was epitomized by a slogan he had seen scrawled on a lorry, 'Vote Maggie and retire at 16'. He dismissed Conservative attempts to blame everything on the world recession as a mere 'perjured alibi'. To thunderous applause he said that the Tory hankering for Victorian values was really hankering for social subservience – hence the attempts to destroy the trade unions. The Conservatives, in their efforts to privatize British Telecom, were like the bandits in the Magnificent Seven, stealing the crop from the growers and selling it to the wealthiest purchaser.

Labour published a succession of leaked Government papers on numerous matters during the election campaign, intending to show that the Government was withholding information from the public which proved that the economy was heading for even deeper recession. However, the production of these 'secret' papers during the weeks of the campaign gradually became self-destructive. The Conservatives, and particularly Cecil Parkinson, were successfully able to dismiss the matter as an indication of how desperate the Labour Party's campaign was growing. While to many in the electorate it seemed a cheap shoddy manoeuvre unworthy of a Party that seriously claimed it wanted to form a government, Kinnock was enthusiastic about the production of these leaked papers.

At a Labour assembly in Manchester he dramatically flourished photocopies of confidential minutes from a National Economic Development Council meeting that had taken place in early March, and that had been anonymously sent to him in a brown envelope.

He stated that the paper, which was a forecast of British economic performance, had been deliberately withheld from publication. The president of the CBI, Sir Campbell Fraser, was minuted as having described the report as 'so gloomy that people reading it would want to get the first boat out of the country'. CBI director general, Sir Terence Beckett, had agreed, and had said, 'publication would not be productive, because there was not a single item of cheer in it'. Sir Geoffrey Howe had also opposed publication of the paper, which he had said should be deferred for a few months to enable more civil service discussion. Kinnock had claimed in his assembly speech that the election was on 9 June 'because the Government has been told by the National Economic Development Council that under present government policies, the slump in Britain could and would only get worse'. Foot supported Kinnock's claim that the paper had been deliberately withheld. As details of the paper were made known, during the week-end, Kinnock's intimation that he had brought it to the attention of the media as evidence of Conservative fiddling began to seem rather absurd, and he was forced onto the defensive. It became apparent that the main justification agreed by ministers, TUC and CBI at the March gathering for not publishing the paper, which was essentially a historical consideration of Britain's industrial performance, was that it would be of help to countries competing with Britain for inward investment. Even Len Murray, the TUC general secretary, had at the time agreed that publication should be deferred.

Historically the Labour leader has generally been more popular than the Labour Party itself. At the beginning of the campaign a BBC survey showed that if Healey had been leader, Labour would have started level with the Conservatives. But Foot had become an albatross; epitomizing the party as old, remote and irrelevant. Labour's failure to sack him in the spring was to prove a costly error. Foot's talk of Gladstone's Midlothian campaign and of Attlee's post-war government meant nothing to the electorate, the mass of whom were aspirants to the middle class. The lack of coherence or credibility in Labour's programme seemed attributable in the public mind to his evasive and muddled thinking. What unfavourable media coverage failed to show was the honourable decent, self-effacing man that Foot was. His apparent lack of will to succeed was intensified when Jill Foot told the media that her husband intended to resign the leadership even if Labour won. Despite his brilliance, he appeared to be absent-minded, unwilling to co-ordinate his party's campaign and oblivious of his own unpopularity. Labour's fight for the general election was directed by the campaign committee, a crowded, disorganized meeting of thirty that assembled each morning at the Walworth Road headquarters to discuss strategy. There was little co-ordination of the presentation of policies, and Foot conciliated but showed no leadership, much to Kinnock's criticism, at the meetings. Kinnock was appalled with the committee's inefficiency.

It was noted by many commentators that during the campaign it was Kinnock who made some of Labour's best speeches. By concentrating on the caring side of Labour's programme, unemployment, the welfare state, and education, he avoided getting caught in arguments on defence and the Common Market. If others had followed his lead, Labour's 14% gap might have been lessened. No party has ever recovered that much in a campaign but the difference between the parties might not have been so marked. Even Mrs Thatcher had warned her party workers that the Conservatives would have a difficult time in the third week. However, Labour's greatest weakness during the election campaign was that it did not present itself as a united party. The Clause 5 meeting had quickly approved the Labour manifesto, 'The New Hope for Britain', that contained the 'golden sentence' apparently covering the Party's differences on defence and the Common Market. This had been essentially a compromise of wording, rather than policy, between the unilateralists such as Foot and Kinnock, and the moderates led by Denis Healey. While public opinion surveys showed that most of the electorate favoured balanced multilateral nuclear disarmament, there was much unease concerning Labour's policy of unilateralism.

Denis Healey, speaking on 16 May, said Polaris would be abandoned if Britain got 'adequate concessions'. Another Labour moderate, Roy Hattersley, had said on the BBC television programme *Question Time* that if the Soviet Union did not produce concessions, a Labour government would have to think again. Journalists from *The Times* had noted a discrepancy between these statements and the wording in the Party manifesto, which had stated that Labour policy was that 'Britain's Polaris force be included in the nuclear disarmament negotiations in which Britain must take part. We will, after consultation, carry through in the lifetime of the next parliament our non-nuclear defence policy.' When asked at the Labour press conference on 24 May if Labour would dispose of Polaris irrespective of Soviet concessions, Foot hedged the question. The media then headlined Labour's lack of a cohesive defence policy. Foot and Healey then agreed a compromise phrase, that within the lifetime of a Labour government it would 'move towards' a non-nuclear strategy, claiming that much would depend on the 'pace' of disarmament talks. Foot thus began to retreat from the absolute commitment to unilateral disarmament. This lack of commitment was certainly not what most Labour activists wanted from their party. As Labour began altering its policy, the CND added to the embarrassment by stating it was holding Labour to its pledge to scrap Polaris within five years.

For Michael Foot, who had built much of his career on unilateral disarmament, the need to retreat from the scrapping of Polaris was a personal and political humiliation. The policy was also an electoral disaster, and public opinion surveys showed that the British electorate were more concerned with Labour's policy of unconditional nuclear disarmament with no concessions, than with any other aspect of its programme. Foot was evasive, appeared insincere on television, and his impatience to avoid questions on nuclear weapons gave the impression that he was attempting to persuade the electorate into voting for a policy with which he had no intention of abiding. On the doorsteps, Kinnock and other canvassers found that unilateralism was the issue that was putting voters off and that the arguments concerning the scrapping of Polaris were making the Labour Party and Foot seem amateurish. In what appeared to have been a naïve gesture, Foot had written to the Soviet Union asking what the Kremlin thought of Labour's nuclear disarmament policy. Labour then lost an enormous amount of credibility by having further consultations on this issue with its shadow Foreign Secretary, Denis Healey, during a general election campaign, only to be told that the Party's main plank of unilaterialism was just not workable. Labour's plight deteriorated further when former Prime Minister Jim Callaghan speaking at his Cardiff constituency, insisted that 'Britain and the West should not dismantle these weapons [their nuclear armouries] for nothing in return. Polaris submarines ... have a further life-span of ten to twelve years and perhaps longer as effective weapons. We should not give them up unilaterally.'

Callaghan's speech created a furious Labour Party squabble, brushed aside by Callaghan who stated that his views were simply 'more in line with the feelings of the ordinary people'. The Labour newspaper *Tribune* then published an article attacking the leading moderates, Healey, Shore, and Hattersley, for deserting the manifesto commitment to abandon nuclear weapons within five years. Kinnock, a staunch unilateralist and a member of CND for many years, tried to avoid the Party squabble. At a meeting in South Wales he said: 'The Labour Party has a non-nuclear defence policy and the Labour government will implement the policy. It means a more secure Britain because it does not involve the weakening of conventional armament.' Speaking on the commercial station TV-am, he said tersely, of Callaghan's speech, that it had not been helpful to Labour's campaign. 'He has a personal opinion and he is entitled to offer it. He must be the best judge of the wisdom of offering it right in the middle of an election campaign.' Kinnock later, in an interview with *Tribune*, said that the effect of Callaghan's speech was to damage Labour's campaign for a week. By the time of the Friday press conference there was a general belief that the nuclear question had already cost Labour the election. The Party general secretary, Jim Mortimer, told an astonished press conference that when the Campaign Committee had met an hour earlier, it had insisted that 'Michael Foot is the leader of the Party, speaks for the Party, and we support the manifesto'. Foot embarrassingly stated that the question of his leadership had not been discussed, but Mortimer's need to volunteer support of Michael Foot showed that Labour was anticipating doubts about his capacity for leadership.

Public opinion poll samples now showed 47% of the electorate likely to vote Conservative, while Labour had dropped to 28%, because of its nuclear policy; the SDP Alliance stood at 23%. The Labour Campaign Committee, seeing that Foot's leadership was an increasing liability, now agreed that Foot should take a quieter role in the campaign and that more prominence should be given to Labour's leading moderate, Denis Healey, assisted by Roy Hattersley and Kinnock, who was of the respectable left. This new format was tried at the start of the third week, at the morning press conference, where Healey led the attack, attempting to show what the Conservatives' 'real programme' was, as devised by Labour HQ from Government leaked papers. The criticisms of the Tories worked. Hattersley was able to throw the Conservatives on the defensive by accusing them of attempting to destroy the National Health Service. This captured the headlines and was one of the most successful attacks of the campaign. It so worried the Conservatives that Mrs Thatcher, who had just returned from the Williamsburg Summit, was forced to state that she had 'no more intention of dismantling the National Health Service than I have of dismantling Britain's defences'.

On 1 June Hattersley, with Kinnock in support, launched Labour's programme for improving work opportunities for young people. Although this was essentially Kinnock's scheme for 16–19-year-olds, he was clearly not considered moderate enough to be placed in sole charge of a significant element of the election programme. He produced figures showing the increase in youth unemployment in the past four years, and said Labour's schemes would bring hope to young school leavers who were living in a mood of cynicism, despair and disillusionment. He said: 'Labour will restore higher education places to their former levels, both for the qualified young people who have had the door shut in their faces by the cuts ... and for adults who need and can use higher education facilities.' Also, as part of this 'Earning for Learning' deal, Labour would establish traineeship courses that, he said, would lead to additional qualifications. Kinnock claimed that Labour's programme for improving opportunities for the young was to be centred on its policy of making the economy grow.

Conservative Employment Secretary Norman Tebbit, speaking at the Tory press conference later that morning, treated Kinnock's plan for giving pocket money to those still at school with much derision. However, he did concede that the unsuitability of the school curriculum made it difficult for some employers to find youngsters who were appropriately educated. Discussing Labour's plans in more detail Tebbit said:

> It does seem a curious idea because they are going to finance it by withdrawing child allowance. That means £6 or £7 out of the mother's housekeeping and then to tax the father on the value of the £25 allowance. What Mr Kinnock is proposing is that the mother should have less housekeeping, the father should have less money and the youngster should get more pocket money, presumably to strengthen family life so he can give his mother some pocket money himself at the end of the week.

As a publicity stunt, Kinnock conducted Labour's education conference from a dilapidated Victorian school near the Chelsea home of Sir Keith Joseph. Several moderate Labour MPs were critical of this and claimed that Kinnock's search for personal publicity was further weakening the unity of the enfeebled Campaign Committee. Kinnock's Learning for Earning scheme seemed just another model of the Conservatives' Youth Training Programme. It was also a Labour admission of failure: while stating that it would cut the dole queue by 2.5 million, Labour was also acknowledging that unemployment was clearly not going to decline so quickly.

At the very start of the election campaign the Tories had attempted to capitalize on the Falklands Factor, but then, deciding it could not improve its already high standing, maintained a dignified silence. It had generally been assumed that Labour would not mention the Falklands, as many of the electorate had been displeased with Labour's conduct during the conflict, when suddenly on 1 June 1983 Kinnock, with no advance consultation with Foot or the Campaign Committee, issued a carefully worded public statement asking for an inquiry into the sinking of the Argentine cruiser *General Belgrano* with the loss of 368 lives. Hattersley was furious with him for bringing the Falklands into the campaign, especially as there had been a Campaign Committee agreement not to use the *Belgrano* issue. Kinnock was sufficiently cautious to avoid making the claim that Mrs Thatcher had ordered the sinking of the *Belgrano* to pre-empt an Argentine withdrawal from the Falkland Islands by peaceful means. He was careful to state that the need for a comprehensive and detailed public inquiry into the sinking came about because many of the circumstances surrounding the incident were 'at the very least, inconsistent and at the very worst, seriously wrong'. He accused Mrs Thatcher of using the 'thirty-year rule' on government secrecy to obscure the facts of the sinking.

Kinnock, who at the time of the conflict had favoured the sending of the task force, was the first senior Labour personality to hint that Mrs Thatcher had deliberately ordered the sinking to prevent a negotiated settlement. The main basis for his criticisms came from information that had just been published, in a book, to the effect that the commander of the submarine, HMS *Conqueror*, which sank the *Belgrano*, stated that the cruiser had been shadowed for more than thirty hours. The impression given by the Government at the time was that the ship had suddenly been located near the war zone, but in the path of an approaching warship squadron, and that the Admiral of the Fleet, Lord Lewin, had asked Mrs Thatcher for orders for the ship to be sunk. The new evidence now showed that the *Belgrano* was moving past the Burdwood Bank, and was on course for her home port of Ushuaia. The Prime Minister was apparently in possession of an intercepted signal ordering Argentine warships to return to port. Kinnock argued in his statement that there were disturbing inconsistencies in the Government's description of the events concerning the attack on the cruiser. He said the Falklands 'should not be an election issue – the judgement and credibility of the Prime Minister is'. With no impartial investigation, the idea would persist that Mrs Thatcher had ordered the sinking to prevent a negotiated settlement. He demanded: 'Why did the War Cabinet refrain from ordering the *Conqueror* to attack the *Belgrano* for over thirty hours and then give the order when the cruiser was on course for its home port? The most feasible answer to this central question appears to be that the British Government sought war when peace was still at least possible, a peace which would have involved complete Argentine withdrawal followed by a negotiated political settlement.'

The demand by Kinnock for an inquiry caused disquiet amongst the electorate and consolidated support for Mrs Thatcher from Tory voters. Although he denied on the BBC *Newsnight* programme, that evening, that the Falklands was an election issue, his moment for choosing to ask for an inquiry seemed like opportunism. There was probably considerable justification for this, as he had not taken much interest in the Falklands at the time of the conflict and, as has been observed, in thirteen years as a Member of Parliament had never taken any interest in non-nuclear defence, and had never voted for the defence estimates. The Government Defence Minister, Michael Heseltine, dismissed the demand for an inquiry, and said Kinnock's charges were a 'disgraceful misrepresentation' of the Government's efforts to achieve a peaceful settlement. At the Conservative press conference Mrs Thatcher was wary when subjected to persistent questioning by journalists about her motives for the sinking. She stated that it would not be in Britain's national interest to give further details of submarine warfare or military espionage. She rejected demands for an inquiry, and several times insisted that the sinking of the *Belgrano* had been necessary to save British lives. She said, 'I cannot stress more strongly that I am greatly relieved that the question you are asking me today is not how it is that one of our aircraft carriers was sunk. Then, my goodness me, there would have been not only an inquiry, but grief on a scale we have not contemplated.' Kinnock said on the *Newsnight* programme that his demand for an inquiry was a personal enterprise. But when pressed he dodged questions and visibly showed a lack of knowledge of military strategy: he could produce no evidence other than previously published facts. At the time of the war, Foot had believed that Mrs Thatcher had had no option but to sink the cruiser. However, in September 1983 Foot, who had not believed that the *Belgrano* was an election issue, said there should now be a Select Committee to consider the sinking.

On the evening of 1 June, some hours from the time when Kinnock had issued his *Belgrano* criticisms, Deputy Leader Denis Healey made his notorious Falklands 'slaughter' speech, that was to have such a damaging effect on the result of the election. Healey, and other senior Labour personalities, had been furious that the Franks Committee had not provided ammunition with which to attack the Conservatives' immense Falklands prestige. With only a week to go until the general election, with the Conservatives maintaining a 15% lead, Healey finally decided to take a gamble;

he would attempt to discredit the Tory 'Falklands Factor'. Healey knew it was a high risk strategy, but Labour's fortunes were so desperate it was worth the effort. Speaking at a crowded meeting at Selly Oak, Birmingham, he said at the end of a long speech that he had not cleared with the Campaign Committee, that Mrs Thatcher had a personality invented by media agencies. He then stated, 'This Prime Minister, who glories in slaughter, who has taken advantage of the superb professionalism of our armed forces in the Falkland Islands, is at this moment lending the military dictatorship in Buenos Aires millions of pounds to buy weapons, including weapons made in Britain, to kill British servicemen with, and that is stupefying hypocrisy.' The speech was broadcast as the main campaign news item on the national television networks that evening. Cecil Parkinson, chairman of the Conservative Party, then said in a statement released from Central Office: 'This must win the prize for the most contemptible statement of the election campaign.'

At the Conservative press conference, the following morning, during which the Prime Minister dismissed Kinnock's demand for a *Belgrano* inquiry, Mrs Thatcher said of the speech: 'It is quite offensive to me in the sense it will have hurt many people in this country. I think it has gone beyond all bounds of public and political decency and given offence to many people.' Foreign Secretary Francis Pym then added, 'It contains the most abusive, most disgraceful, most unforgivable allegations I have ever heard in any election.' Foot was embarrassed by the remarks, and senior members of the Labour team, angry that Healey should have deflected the Labour campaign from its major theme of unemployment, put immense pressure on Healey to withdraw the statement, which was considered a vote loser. That evening, when appearing on the BBC programme *Question Time*, Healey gracefully conceded that the word 'slaughter' had been a mistake, and said the word he should have used was 'conflict'. 'Conflict' was the term that Healey's wife had used that morning on breakfast television. The Labour deputy leader had thus stood his ground on the substance of his speech, but the Conservatives were able to capitalize on the fact that it took twenty-four hours to withdraw the offending word 'slaughter'.

Healey's gamble for votes was a serious blunder. The one issue on which the whole country was united was that during the Falklands War Mrs Thatcher had done well for Britain. Nowhere was this feeling more strong than among the working people, the very gut of Labour's support. Millions of ordinary working people, who would never vote Conservative, agreed with Mrs Thatcher's Falklands action. Healey, by choosing to denigrate the only issue on which working people were in sympathy with the Conservatives, effectively isolated Labour from its own voters.

Because Foot was considered an electoral liability, Healey had been given more prominence as a voice of moderation. Now he had embarrassed the Party, and his arguments gave Labour the taint of a loser. This image was not helped when Foot himself spoke of the troubles of the Labour leadership. On a Radio 4 programme he said it was a valid argument that the Party had too many intellectuals and that the leadership had lost its working-class origins, adding that Kinnock would be a good Labour leader.

Within a week of Healey's 'slaughter' speech, Kinnock caught Labour in a fresh storm concerning the Falklands, when he said it was a pity that soldiers had to die to prove that Mrs Thatcher had guts. He was speaking on the afternoon of 6 June, during a televised debate, for the TVS station. During the programme the presenter, Llew Gardiner, asked the panel if there was an argument that the election had proved to be about the character and force of Mrs Thatcher's personality and the nation's view of the Falklands conflict. Kinnock's answer was that, until the Falklands conflict, she had been the most loathed Prime Minister in modern history. A member of the invited, but largely hostile, studio audience shouted 'But Mrs Thatcher's got guts'. Kinnock replied, 'And it's a pity that other people had to leave theirs on the ground at Goose Green in order to prove it.' Above the howls of anger from the audience at this comment, he tried to calm the mob:

Now then, now then. The test of a leader of a democratic country includes the ability to lead that country in times of crisis, and I have no wish to detract from her efforts, but do not let us confuse her arrogance with any particular form of strength or the fact that she was ruthless with her party and cabinet. Do not let us fall into the trap of voting for a schoolyard bully because if we develop a one-person Government as we have had in the last year we will deserve to live on our knees.

Soon there was condemnation of Kinnock's remarks, which were broadcast that evening. The Defence Secretary, Michael Heseltine, speaking at a meeting in Swansea, described him as 'the self-appointed king of the gutter. He has spent so much of his time in the vicious back-biting world of the left wing that he has forgotten the basic standards of human decency.' Tebbit accused Healey and Kinnock of 'trawling the gutters for filth', and condemned Labour for their 'campaign of dirt and deceit'. Dr David Owen stated that Foot should make Kinnock withdraw the remark immediately, and said, 'The country should not have to wait twenty-four hours for a half-hearted retraction.'

Kinnock's careless talk had been a major political blunder, made worse because Labour was now in the last week of the election campaign. At Labour headquarters his remarks caused alarm: they were seen as being in poor taste and of no help to the Party. Kinnock was trapped. If he retreated and withdrew his comments, it would have been a humiliating recognition that Tory and SDP criticisms were justified – it would also have contributed to Labour's image for altering what it said. If he did not withdraw his statement, or attempt to alter its meaning, he would be accused of lack of concern for the suffering of those who had fought. Timing was also critical as 7 June was the anniversary of Bluff Cove, when thirty-six Welsh Guardsmen died on the landing-ship *Sir Galahad*.

From the TVS studio Kinnock went to spend what was left of the campaign in South Wales. Journalists telephoned him at his home in Pontllanfraith but he would not budge on what he had said, stating only that he deeply shared the grief of bereaved families who had lost soldiers in the Falklands. Meanwhile, at the local Labour Party headquarters, telephone messages from the Falklands relatives had started to arrive. But to Kinnock's agent, Barry Moore, who was answering the telephones, the pattern was immediately clear: Welsh families were unanimously in favour of what Kinnock had said. Kinnock then thought of a scheme which was to be a brilliant political move. By chance he was on the list to appear at the Wales Labour Party news conference at Cardiff on the morning of 7 June. At the television conference Kinnock said he had no regrets about his impromptu remarks but was concerned that servicemen's families should not be distressed: that he was personally writing to each of the families of those killed or injured. He then made known the contents of the letter he was sending:

Publicity has, as you know, been given recently to impromptu remarks which I made on a television programme.

I do not know what version of the remarks you have heard from the journalists who have contacted you on June 6th but the enclosed cutting from the 'Western Mail' on June 7th is the most accurate which I have seen in print and both ITN and BBC gave a full filmed version of the remarks in news and current affairs programmes on June 6th.

The accurate record of those remarks makes it clear that they were unpremeditated and were said without any intention of hurting the families whose loved ones were either killed or wounded in the Falklands campaign. I would never – consciously or unconsciously – add to the anguish felt during and since that War. Nor would I say or do anything that could be interpreted in any way as disloyalty to the armed servicemen and civilian personnel engaged in the Conflict. They fulfilled their task with great bravery and efficiency and no one, certainly not I, could or would, diminish their sacrifice or their service.

My remarks in response to a shouted interruption on that television programme were directed at the Prime Minister. It is the plain fact of history that her conduct following the invasion of the Falkland Islands and throughout the subsequent weeks of fighting gained her a reputation for fortitude to which the interrupter was apparently referring. I honestly felt then and continue to honestly feel now that it was and is a pity – a tragic pity – that with or without her intervention, the Prime Minister's reputation was advanced through such sacrifice. Indeed I think it probable that Mrs Thatcher like any responsible person would prefer to succeed in any activity without loss of life and without injury or pain.

I can understand the initial reaction to any remarks which in their reporting or misreporting might have appeared to give the impression of callousness to people like you who have suffered the loss or injury of your men. I hope that the accurate record will remove any such impression since I have nothing but respect for the way in which they and their comrades did their duty.

Yours sincerely,
Neil Kinnock

With considerable pugnaciousness Kinnock, by sending the letter, not only stood by what he had said, but went further and elaborated his statement. The Tory claim that his words were offensive to the families of those who had been killed was swept aside. He had even gone one better than Mrs Thatcher, and sent a long letter of condolence to every family of the Falklands dead, which Mrs Thatcher had never done. The genius of Kinnock's letter was that he had allowed his accusation of Mrs Thatcher to stand, without taking any of the criticism. At the main Labour Party news conference Foot refused to condemn Kinnock, but instead said, 'When I am invited to condemn what Neil Kinnock said by people like David Owen or Michael Heseltine I'm all the more determined to do no such thing.' He added, with some justification, that he wished the media had given one hundredth of the space they had devoted to Kinnock's statement to the campaign he had been waging against youth unemployment. Among senior Labour personalities no attempt was made to make Kinnock withdraw his statement.

Having issued the letter, Kinnock spoke on the telephone from the local Transport Union district office to some of the families. During one such conversation with a father whose son had died on the *Sir Galahad*, Kinnock broke down in tears, and wept as he described the conversation to journalists. Later in the morning, during a series of walkabouts in Cardiff, he was given a varied but generally favourable hearing. At an open air public meeting, when asked what he thought of Mr Heseltine's 'king of the gutter' accusation, he said, 'If I was in the gutter, and I ain't, he'd still be looking up at me from the sewer.' At the party headquarters in Cardiff, during the week, the phones were going virtually the whole time, and every message from Welsh people was in agreement with what he had said. However, elsewhere in the country people thought very differently, and Kinnock was sent numerous threats.

Although the 'guts at Goose Green' speech had increased Kinnock's own popularity in South Wales, it was none the less a political blunder that was to contribute to Labour's humiliating defeat at the general election. For the second time in a week, the first being the *Belgrano* statement, Kinnock had, although not purposefully, advanced his own standing within the Party at the price to Labour of electoral disaster. Although there were clearly no general election votes to be won in personal attacks on Mrs Thatcher, Labour was now sniffing defeat and Tory criticism did Kinnock's standing within the Party no harm. Within hours of issuing the Goose Green letter Kinnock launched the most fiery, vitriolic, and thundering attack on the Conservatives of the whole of Labour's campaign. Speaking to an audience in Glamorgan, on the evening of 7 June, and evoking the spectre of 1984, he said:

I WARN YOU that you will have ignorance, when talents are untended and wits are wasted, when learning is a privilege and not a right.

I WARN YOU that you will be cold when fuel charges are used as a tax system that the rich don't notice and the poor can't afford.

I WARN YOU that you must not expect work – when many cannot spend, more will not be able to earn. When they don't earn, they don't spend. When they don't spend, work dies.

I WARN YOU not to go into the streets alone after dark or into the streets in large crowds of protest in the light.

I WARN YOU that you will be quiet, when the curfew of fear and the gibbet of unemployment make you obedient.

I WARN YOU that you will have defence of a sort with a risk and at a price that passes all understanding.

I WARN YOU that you will be home-bound when fares and transport bills kill leisure and lock you up.

I WARN YOU that you will borrow less, when credit, loans, mortgages and easy payments are refused to people on your melting income.

If Margaret Thatcher wins on Thursday, she will be more a leader than a Prime Minister. That power produces arrogance and when it is toughened by Tebbitry and flattened and fawned upon by spineless sycophants, the boot-licking tabloid knights of Fleet Street and place-men in the quangos, the arrogance corrupts absolutely.

If Margaret Thatcher wins on Thursday, I warn you not to be ordinary, I warn you not to be young, I warn you not to fall ill, I warn you not to get old.

Having spent Wednesday evening at a large eve-of-election meeting at his constituency, and most of Thursday 9 June campaigning, on Thursday evening Kinnock went to London to appear on the various television 'election special' programmes. As the count at his own constituency was not to be until Friday afternoon, he had the unique advantage – for Labour – of being able to appear in the studios of the national television media on election night. No other senior Labour politician was able to do this, because there were no safe constituencies near London. Kinnock thus had the good fortune to be the television spokesman on the BBC 'election special' programme: he said that the lessons of Labour's civil war 'have not been lost on the Labour Party, but it is perhaps that they were not learnt quickly enough'. When asked if he was anticipating being leader of the Labour Party, he answered, 'Mr Foot is the leader of the Labour Party, and until he makes a declaration to the contrary, speculation, I think, is somewhat foolhardy.' Hattersley had been successful at his Birmingham constituency, and against the national trend in favour of the Conservatives, he had increased his own majority. Interviewed at his constituency election count, he cautiously distanced himself from the election manifesto that was sacred to Labour activists and party workers. When asked if he thought there would have been a less unfavourable general election with a leader other than Michael Foot, Hattersley stated that the leadership question was a matter only for Michael Foot.

Such was Labour's sense of humiliation that many of the party workers at Walworth Road headquarters did not even watch the results on television. A personal tragedy for Kinnock was the defeat of Joan Lestor. As had happened to him, Lestor had been attacked in her constituency for not voting for Tony Benn in the deputy leadership contest. Kinnock, having dashed from the studios of the BBC to appear as a guest on ITN's *Election Special*, was asked by Alastair Burnet what blame he took for Labour's disaster, and was he sorry about the campaign. Kinnock blamed the views of the press that had mobilized itself against Labour, and claimed that the origins of defeat had been sown during the past two or three years by certain elements of the Party that had made victory difficult. He said, 'The British people, or sections of the British people, voted to live on their knees and we're going to lift them off that.'

The defeat of Tony Benn at Bristol was of great significance to Kinnock. The minimum qualification in an election for Party leader was that candidates had to be Members of Parliament. Kinnock would now have a clear chance in the future leadership contest if Foot resigned, but on television he was magnanimous, showing no emotion. He said of Benn, 'He has been the object of a longer and thicker, sustained barrage of abuse than any other politician in the land. Probably only Michael Foot rivals him for the kind of assassination that has taken place, and it is sad that the voters of that constituency were sufficiently impressed by that to have caused Tony's defeat.' But Kinnock was also quick to apportion what he saw to be Benn's responsibility for Labour's failure. He said that the deputy leadership contest wounded the Party and that 'the consequences went to the root of British politics and are partly the reason for the kind of condition we are in'. This was a curious statement from Kinnock, who during the general election campaign had spoken more class hatred and made more personal attacks than anyone else in the Labour Party.

Michael Foot said on the programme that the fight for another general election had to start immediately. With the knowledge that Tony Benn had been defeated, and the field was clear for Kinnock, he looked noticeably chirpy when asked about the leadership. 'I'm not making any prophesies', he said. There would have to be discussions about the task of reconstructing the Party. 'We have got to learn from this defeat.' Minutes later the Tories achieved an absolute majority and had won the general election.

7 · Leader

Labour had suffered its most humiliating defeat in sixty years. On 9 June the Conservatives won 397 seats, Labour 209, the Social Democrats 6, and the Liberals 17. Labour's defeat was so disastrous that if the Party were to continue to decline at the same rate it would cease to be a force in British politics. It had won 8.5 million votes, or the support of only 27% of the electorate, which was 10% less than its post-war low of 36.9% in 1979. Even during Labour's wilderness period in the 1950s when it lost three elections it never polled less than 43% of the vote. What the June result meant was that of those entitled to vote, only one in five had supported Labour. A survey done by the *Observer* found that between 1945 and 1983 the gap between the main parties, even in the election landslides of 1959 and 1966, was never greater than 10%. The margin in June 1983 of 15% was so great that the Conservatives could be deserted by one in four of their voters and still have a majority at a general election. Labour had just lost a staggering 119 deposits, against a total of 82 in eleven post-war general elections. To win in the future, it would need a swing of 13%, and no party had achieved that since 1945. It would also need to recapture 120 seats, which appeared to be almost impossible, since it was second in only 132 seats, and third or fourth in 292 seats. South of a line from Cardiff to Grimsby, but excluding London, Labour had won only three seats. Of those, it had only been possible to win Ipswich by keeping off policy and omitting the word 'Labour' from the election leaflet. The Party's traditional strength of working-class voters had deserted in their millions, and Labour had failed to appeal to the affluent working classes and the new middle classes. On 9 June Labour could claim the loyalty of just 35% of manual workers (down 12% since 1979), 47% of the unskilled (down 11%), and 38% of trade unionists (down 14%). Most of the young voters had ignored Labour. Of the three million unemployed, whose votes had seemed assured, less than half had voted Labour. This was a damning failure of Kinnock's education policy, with its priority for youth training. It had even been rejected by those people whom it was supposed to help.

On the morning of 10 June Neil and Glenys travelled to South Wales to attend the count at Kinnock's own constituency. The voters of Islwyn cast 23,183 votes for Kinnock, and he thus had a comfortable majority of 14,380 over his SDP opponent, the Conservatives achieving 5,511 votes. In previous general elections he had fought, he had consistently achieved majorities of over 21,000; the apparent slump in his vote was accounted for by boundary changes and a heavy swing to the Social Democrats. As he was now being tipped as a future leader, he was besieged by the press when, after the count, he took Glenys for a celebratory pint of beer at the local pub.

With Labour's general election humiliation, it was understood among senior Labour personalities that Foot would state his intention to resign at the Wednesday 15 June meeting of the Parliamentary Labour Party. It was believed that he would either resign immediately, thus having Denis Healey as a caretaker leader until a leadership election at the autumn conference, or more likely he would stand down at the conference. Whatever happened, it was known that nominations for a leadership contest would have to be sent in by 15 July, and if there was to be a leadership election it would be at the Party conference, in four months' time. Foot had planned to inform the Parliamentary Labour Party meeting that he would be stepping down in October. A widespread Fleet Street assumption at the time was that, with Tony Benn no longer an MP, the favourite for the leadership would be Denis Healey, because of his considerable ministerial knowledge. However, Fleet Street, which for several years had been criticizing the Labour Party civil war, had seen the proliferation of the left, but had forgotten the logic of its own arguments. It was precisely because power in the Labour Party had shifted down to the grassroots, especially in the form of the 30-40-30 idea, giving 30% to the PLP and the constituencies and 40% to the trade unions, that it was impossible for a candidate other than one from the broad left to be elected leader.

Meanwhile, the trade unions were disgruntled. The £2¼ million which Trade Unions for a Labour Victory (TLV) had scraped together for the election, the Party, led by Michael Foot, had effectively just tipped down the drain. Labour's defeat was bad news for the unions, who were themselves now seriously in decline: their total membership had dropped by 10% since 1979 as a consequence of the economic recession. The Labour Party had even failed in the original purpose for which it was established in the 1900s, which was to get elected to represent trade union parliamentary interests. Labour's defeat meant that the Thatcher government was free to pass legislation curbing union influence even further. The trade union leadership widely attributed Labour's poor results to bitter divisions within the Party, while there was now some pressure from right-wing unions for alterations in policies which had proved unacceptable to the electorate. On 10 June David Basnett, chairman of TLV, hinted at criticism of Foot when he said, 'the leadership issue has to be clarified as quickly as possible'. A TLV meeting had been arranged for 13 June, when it was thought the unions would lobby for a leadership candidate of the centre right, such as Hattersley, Shore, or Healey.

During the morning of 12 June the council of the white-collar union ASTMS met to agree to nominate Foot for reselection as leader at the Labour Party conference. However, it was agreed that if Foot wished to stand down it would offer the nomination to Kinnock. The general secretary of ASTMS, Clive Jenkins, telephoned Foot and offered him the nomination but Foot said that he would not be standing. Jenkins then telephoned the BBC *World This Weekend* studio urgently demanding to speak to Kinnock who was being interviewed in a discussion on the general election. Jenkins asked Kinnock whether, as Foot was resigning, he would accept the ASTMS nomination for the Labour leadership. Kinnock said that he would, and Jenkins then promptly informed the Press Association that Michael Foot was going and that ASTMS were supporting Kinnock. Thus even before the news had been issued of Foot's resignation, Kinnock was assured of the 147,000 votes from one of the largest trade unions.

Foot and his aides were furious that Jenkins had leaked news of the resignation, making what should have been a dignified stepping down from the leadership seem a squalid and hustled operation. Jenkins, however, maintained he had Foot's permission to make the announcement. Interviewed on *The World This Weekend*, Jenkins said ASTMS were nominating Kinnock because he was a 'young and sophisticated politician' with 'dash, sparkle, imagination, persuasive quality', who would work well not only with the unions but with the constituencies. Speaking on the programme, Kinnock said that he would accept the nomination for the leadership with 'gratitude', and that he was daunted by the prospect of leadership, but not frightened. He was, however, cautious not to confine himself to the leadership contest and suggested that he might also have to stand for the deputy leadership. He then issued a statement giving his purposes for wanting to lead the Party. He claimed these were: to attack and defeat the Conservatives by every democratic means; to sustain the energy and cohesion which Labour had shown in the general election campaign; and to show the people in Britain that Labour's democratic socialist policies were the modern, practical means of achieving security, prosperity and justice for the country.

Kinnock was now badly fatigued after his gruelling general election touring, but as Foot had confirmed that he was resigning he had no choice but to contest the leadership immediately. However, whereas other candidates were just beginning their campaigns, Kinnock had already as good as won his. He was now reaping the advantages of his years of energetic dashing about the country, often on seemingly worthless visits, getting himself known in obscure wards and constituencies. Trade union leaders were now scrambling to give him their support. During late Sunday afternoon the general council of the TGWU, Britain's largest trade union, agreed to support Kinnock if Foot did not wish to be nominated. For Kinnock the 1.25 million TGWU votes was a massive foundation that was 8% of the total electoral franchise. He was then promised union nominations from the leaders of Sogat '82 and the Communication Workers' Union. By the evening it was made known that Healey would not be contesting the leadership and might be stepping down as deputy leader. Healey had been badly shaken by the abuse that had been hurled at him for his 'glorying in slaughter' speech and, at sixty-five, believed he was too old to try for the leadership. Shore and Hattersley had stated their intentions to challenge for the leadership, and Heffer said that he would also be making a bid. It was, however, clear that the strongest contest was going to be between Kinnock and Hattersley. Yet only hours from the beginning of the contest Kinnock was already far ahead and the clear favourite, being quoted at 6–4 by Coral's, the bookmakers. Not only had Kinnock much trade union support, but he also had the approval of the tabloid Fleet Street newspapers, traditionally read by Labour working-class voters. The mood of Labour thinking at the week-end moved strongly against the old-established generation of Labour Party leaders. On Monday 13 June the *Daily Star* stated that 'Labour now needs a strong, tough, angry young leader who will rebuild, rethink and reorganize the Party'. The *Daily Mirror* leader article stated that Labour needed a winner: 'Now the party should look for someone younger, some-one who could be in charge for as long as Sir Harold Wilson.'

The trade unions' flurry of invitations to nominate Kinnock conformed with his image of apparently unambitious success with no effort. Despite his quiet confidence of winning on the first count, and his tiredness after the general election, it was necessary to arrange a campaign. He spoke to Robin Cook, aged thirty-seven, a leading Tribunite defence spokesman and unilateralist, inviting him to be his campaign manager. With Kinnock now emerging as the future leader, half the Parliamentary Labour Party wanted to be members of the Kinnock campaign team. However, the team was limited in size, consisting of Kinnock, his secretary Maureen Willis, education assistant Charles Clarke, Cook, and Kinnock's parliamentary education spokesmen, Alf Dubs and Frank Dobson. A district system was then devised whereby MPs would monitor the campaigning in groups of constituencies. At the first campaign meeting on 13 June the team used Kinnock's speaking diary to add on more tours and develop a programme of district speaking. Financing of the campaign was to be by donation and letters were published in *Tribune* and *Labour Weekly*, asking for financial help. The immediate concern of Kinnock and his team was to see that the four-month leadership contest did not harm the Party: discus-sions were therefore held with Hattersley's campaign team to this effect, and by the end of the contest it was agreed that Labour had not greatly suffered. A low-profile campaign was certainly beneficial to Kinnock, as the team knew that his greatest electoral asset was his personality; anything that avoided discussion on policy was to be welcomed. It was not until July that Kinnock issued an election leaflet, by which time he had got the votes he needed to win.

As Healey would not be standing in October, the contest had also begun for the deputy leadership. Michael Meacher, aged forty-three a lieutenant of Tony Benn's, stated that he would be standing for the deputy leadership, as were Gwyneth Dunwoody, and Gerald Kaufman. The media suggested speculation on the American idea of a 'dream ticket' combining Kinnock for leader and Hattersley for deputy, or vice versa, but neither candidate was keen on this idea as it suggested failure. However, with the help of some delicate negotiations by the campaign managers, both candidates simultaneously issued almost identical statements, that they would be standing for the deputy leadership as well as the leadership positions. Kinnock in his statement said he was standing for the leadership with no reservation: however, 'as a contribution to Labour unity', he was willing to accept nominations for the deputy leadership.

The goodwill that Kinnock had cultivated among the Labour movement was now evident: trade unions stampeded to offer their support. While the 30-40-30 franchise gave 40% of the votes in the leadership contest to the trade unions, no procedures had been established to ensure that the unions adequately consulted their members. The mass of union support that had been assured to Kinnock in the first week of the campaign had mostly just been in the form of personal guarantees from union general secretaries. The suspicions of Labour moderates were alerted by media stories of a conversation among a large group of union leaders during a reception given by the American Ambassador on 13 June, who were overheard saying whom their union delegations would be supporting, even before consulting their own memberships.

Kinnock had won many friends among the trade union leadership during his speaking tours at union conferences, and his popularity was helped by his gift for winning the admiration of people older than himself. Although the campaign was to last fifteen weeks, by the first week he had assurances of nomination from ASTMS, Sogat '82, TGWU, USDAW, UCW, and ASLEF. By 27 June Kinnock had the support of unions representing more than 3.8 million trade unionists against Hattersley's 1.8 million. These nominations were verified in a whole series of summer conferences and special union council meetings; union leaders, realizing that their earlier hasty nominations appeared to be undemocratic, readily approved these meetings.

Despite the deluge of votes that Kinnock attracted, many commentators, still thinking in terms of the party of the Harold Wilson era, were sceptical that Kinnock could win. Until late June the deputy editor of the *Observer*, Anthony Howard, continued to believe that Hattersley would be leader. What had surprised most commentators was Kinnock's popularity among MPs; due to the leftward shift of the Parliamentary Labour Party. Once about a third of the PLP had been broad left, but now in the new parliament, the figure was nearly half. In early July the Kinnock team believed that on the basis of their canvass of the 209 Labour MPs, their candidate could be certain of the votes of at least 120–125. Kinnock was especially popular among younger Labour MPs because he appeared to show that it was possible to achieve high office in the Labour Party despite not having been a minister. He was also admired by the constituency parties and MPs of the broad left for his determined belief that there was no need to alter Labour's programme. The constituencies were his great strength: he had assiduously cultivated them in his years of speaking tours, accumulating debts of honour. He had won the support of the young broad left group, the Labour Co-ordinating Committee, which agreed that Labour's policies only needed modifying to make them more acceptable to the electorate, and said it would be willing to campaign for Kinnock. Such was his popularity amongst the constituencies that when his campaign team made their survey in late July, it found that he could anticipate winning 75% of the constituency section.

A MORI survey during the third week of June showed that of Labour voters sampled on the matter of the leadership, 56% favoured Kinnock, 27% Hattersley, 16% Shore, and only 1%

Heffer. However, this survey was also bad news for Labour, as it found that amongst those traditional Labour supporters who had voted Conservative or SDP at the general election, 45% were now in favour of Hattersley, and only 30% backed Kinnock. This disparity was not as great as that in the 1980 Healey–Foot contest, but it appeared to show a crucial disadvantage for Labour in choosing Kinnock as leader. It was among precisely these voters that Labour would need to find a 13% swing if it was to win another general election.

Among the Party's leading centre-right moderates, Kinnock was personally liked and his qualities such as his great capacity to be a 'good listener' were acknowledged. Even the chief scourge of the left, John Golding, stated that Kinnock had the essential characteristic of a leader, which was the gift of being acceptable to ordinary working people. However, although he was personally popular among moderate Labour MPs, there was disagreement with him on policy, and indignation at his rapid success. Others were envious, especially former ministers, practical realists, who disliked Kinnock's ability to further himself without ever having taken government office. In terms of policies the moderates felt that it was beyond comprehension how anyone as intelligent as Kinnock obviously was, could fail to see that Labour had lost the election because of the Party's unpopular policies and remote leadership. Kinnock's failure to appreciate that seemed to stress his careerist ambition. Even moderate trade union leaders believed that these Labour policies had been the prime cause of the Party's election defeat. Some moderates, who saw Kinnock as just a younger Michael Foot, determined to adhere to the same unappealing policies, believed that his leadership would be deleterious for the Party. There was speculation that if Kinnock was unable to revive Labour's fortunes fifty moderate MPs would form a new Democratic Labour Party.

Kinnock had been able to win no support among the shadow cabinet which almost entirely favoured Roy Hattersley. Hattersley's campaign was headed by Denis Healey supporters, and Healey himself wrote to the *News of the World* stating that Hattersley should be Labour's candidate as there was no time 'for a long process of learning by trial and error'. Hattersley, by concentrating on the practicalities of Labour's programme, disagreed with Kinnock on the fundamental issues of unilateralism and the Common Market, and stated that Labour had lost in June because its policies lacked credibility and it had ceased to listen to the voters. The Hattersley team believed that their candidate should make his appeal on the basis of his experience as a government minister, which was considered to be his greatest strength. However, Hattersley had never been a noticeably competent minister; when he was at the Foreign Office officials had sometimes found him hesitant and indecisive. But perhaps his competence or casualness were both irrelevant for the new Labour Party professed widespread disinterest in government ministerial know-how. Indeed Kinnock was popular among the constituencies precisely because he had not been tainted by government office. His popularity within the Party had been underestimated by the moderates in the unions and the constituencies who were bewildered and frustrated at attempts by the broad left heirs of Michael Foot to secure the leadership for Kinnock by means that disregarded the need for wider consultation.

What had been claimed by the entire spectrum of those concerned with the leadership contest, from the Bennite left, the Heffer and Shore campaigns, to the Hattersley centre-right, was that the trade unions had been pledging their nominations to Kinnock amongst others before consultation with their grassroots membership. A comment made at the time by an official of the Hattersley campaign team, Dr John Cunningham, was that, 'It is grotesque to be lectured about the future of the Labour Party by communist trade union leaders and then see our individual members excluded from the decisions.' There was also the argument that there should be wider consultation in the constituency parties. It was forgotten that Kinnock had for years favoured voting on wider franchises, at every level of the Labour Party. As early as December 1980 he had tabled an NEC motion suggesting that there should be a provision in the Party constitution for local general management committees, during a leadership contest, to consult their membership. However, during the 1983 leadership contest, he kept noticeably quiet. Heffer wrote to each trade union asking for the 'widest democratic involvement of the membership' in the leadership contest. He attacked the media for their coverage of the leadership election, saying: 'This is a Labour Party election, and whoever becomes the leader and deputy leader, it must be decided by the membership of the Party and not by the television and the press.' Shore had also asked for union general secretaries to consult their members and stated that, in the constituencies, there should be a system of one member one vote. Already, however, so many nominations had been promised to Kinnock, that the plight of his rivals was hopeless.

Heffer and Shore were genuinely concerned that the position of Kinnock as a future leader would be weakened if his election was seen to have been made a formality by union leaders, but there was also the naïve belief by the Heffer and Shore campaigns that if they could only just appeal directly to the grassroots union membership they would win more nominations. Nothing, however, could have been more wrong. What was so remarkable about Kinnock's popularity with the trade unions was that it was not just confined to the leadership. As a MORI *Sunday Times* survey demonstrated, he was also the popular choice among the trade union grassroots. This was indeed the great strength of his claim to leadership: he did have the support of every sector of the Party, from the trade unionists to the constituency parties, and of most of the MPs. The MORI survey, published on 3 July, showed that 35% of trade union members favoured Kinnock and 28% Hattersley. The survey also found that a large sector of trade unionists – 70% – favoured a postal count to decide who should be the Labour leader. Kinnock's widespread popularity among trade unionists became increasingly evident during the campaign as the unions gradually consulted their branch and shop-floor members and found them overwhelmingly in favour of Kinnock. Hattersley had been depending upon his nomination by the public employees' union NUPE. However, when this union received its members' votes, it found there was massive support for Kinnock. Such was the Kinnock campaign team's confidence in their candidate's popularity that when unions consulted their membership they did not anticipate losing a single nomination.

The apparently cosy 'dream ticket' idea of the moderates' campaign for Hattersley and the broad left campaign by Kinnock was damaged on 21 July by comments made by Hattersley at a Parliamentary Labour Party meeting. At an earlier, angry meeting of the shadow cabinet, a motion had been considered that during the leadership elections the constituency parties and trade unions should consult their membership as much as possible. Kinnock and Heffer were against putting this to the PLP for discussion; Foot was sceptical, disliking the idea of the Parliamentary party suggesting guidelines to the trade unions and local parties. Kinnock, Heffer and Foot were decisively defeated by 12 votes to 3. The shadow cabinet now decided that the motion should be put to the PLP meeting the following evening. Foot adhered to this majority decision and went to the meeting, intending to do his duty as leader and speak for the wider franchise motion in terms that would not offend the trade unions. However, at the PLP meeting a resolution was passed that the meeting should move to another item on the agenda, and thus there should be no discussion on the consultation motion. Foot did nothing to stop this and abstained in the voting. The shadow cabinet, especially those supporting Roy Hattersley, were furious that Foot had not used his authority to ensure discussion of a wider franchise. Accounts of what followed have varied, but the substance was that Hattersley muttered aloud, 'We have been betrayed. Where's the leadership now?' No one appeared to take any notice until, as the meeting ended, Foot went over to Hattersley and shouted at him 'Don't you ever talk to me like that again'.

A Hattersley supporter, Joe Ashton, claimed that supporters of Kinnock, and especially those of Heffer and Meacher, had deliberately packed the PLP meeting and 'bounced' the vote. This was the view of many moderate MPs who believed that Kinnock and his supporters were determined to limit the franchise as much as possible. The idea had continued that Kinnock's election was a covenant of the unrepresentative constituency activists, broad left trade unionists, and the Bevanite leadership of Michael Foot. As Foot was making his last appearance at the PLP as leader it seemed as though his final act had been to clear the path for Kinnock as his chosen successor.

While senior MPs of both campaigns were now claiming that there was no prospect of their candidates' serving as leader and deputy leader, the campaign teams were determined to ensure a clean fight and minimize the damage to the Party. Kinnock, who had been on his campaign tour, had not been at the PLP meeting. Speaking at the Welsh Labour Party conference on 23 July 1983 at Llandrindod Wells, he was conciliatory, and said that he would be pleased to work with Hattersley, but ominously warned his audience that he considered those who put their own 'fortune above the interests of the movement with great impatience'. Kinnock never made his thoughts on voting on a wider franchise clear during the campaign, until early August, by which time he had safely won as many nominations as he needed; he then stated in a letter to *Labour Weekly* that he was in favour of the widest possible consultations of the Party membership during a leadership contest. Despite this, he was opposed to the idea of interference with the internal democracies of the trade unions, which he claimed was merely assisting the Conservatives, and stated that discussions concerning wider franchises could only be theoretical as there was no prospect of making constitutional alterations until the Labour Party conference.

The parliamentary argument had done Hattersley an injustice. His swearing at Foot was a blunder as idiotic as Kinnock's 'guts at Goose Green' attack on Mrs Thatcher. Although an electoral disaster, Foot, the old campaigner, was loved and revered by constituency party workers, and admired by most trade union leaders. Hattersley's insult to this revered old warrior probably cost his fight for the leadership more votes than was appreciated at the time. The Kinnock campaign team believed that the disrespectful comment was 'a bit like hitting your own granny'.

Hattersley's campaign was now beginning to appear desperate. While Kinnock's success had appeared to be effortless, Hattersley lost much prestige by appearing to try. He was even shown on the *Nationwide* programme travelling by rail to an obscure trade union conference at Llandudno, writing his speech in the luggage van. Hattersley's uncharacteristically aggressive campaigning seemed increasingly hopeless, and gave him the air of a loser. Traditionally the Labour moderates had been the best organized in the Party but now Kinnock's presidential style of campaigning impressed many by its efficiency. The Kinnock team had acquired a word processor that was used for sending out papers, while the Hattersley team were unable even to get a proper list of the trade unions and had to distribute papers by hand. Hattersley concentrated on a more 'popularist' campaign, advocating the sale of council houses and, while disagreeing with little in the Labour manifesto, arguing that the Party had lost the general election, and five million voters, because its programme had ceased to be credible. As Hattersley's campaign seemed lost by early July, he increasingly concentrated his attention on the battle for the deputy leadership.

The defeat of Tony Benn at the general election had shocked the far left, many of whom had never forgiven Kinnock for organizing a coup several years earlier to stop Benn's attempt at the deputy leadership. In June 1983 Kinnock was even described in the far left journal, *London Labour Briefing*, edited by Ken Livingstone, as a 'preaching careerist'. The far left did not therefore support Kinnock and once satisfied that Hattersley was not going to win the leadership, contributed their token support to Eric Heffer. This did not worry Kinnock as his popularity was such that he did not need the votes of the far left; this was significant for it meant that if elected, he would owe them nothing and so could deal with them as he wished.

Although the deputy leadership had little constitutional significance, it was a public demonstration of the Labour Party's attitude of mind, and it was to secure this job that the far left now directed its attention. By August the far left's candidate, Meacher, looked as though he would beat Hattersley for the deputy's job. While the claims of the Meacher campaign team were later proven to have been distorted, it was believed at the time that Meacher could win as much as 81% of the constituency vote. With these and several major union nominations favouring Meacher, it looked as if Hattersley might even fail to win the deputy leadership. This led to speculation concerning a further defection of moderate Labour MPs from the Party to the SDP. Hattersley stated that Labour could not win another general election with a Kinnock–Meacher leadership, and warned, with Denis Healey, that he would no longer bother to stand for the shadow cabinet. Kinnock professed not to take sides on the matter of the deputy leadership, but was not keen on the idea of the Bennite, Meacher, as his possible deputy. This was made clear during September when, in a notorious interview with Jilly Cooper, Kinnock made such disparaging comments of Meacher that they were to contribute to the Bennite's defeat.

Although Kinnock seemed certain to win, his campaign now suffered an apparent disaster. With the battle for the leadership only a week old, Kinnock was ordered by his doctor to rest his voice. The form of laryngitis that he had caught during the general election, which had caused him voice strain, had worsened. He was ordered not to speak publicly for at least a month to avoid permanent damage to his voice. He was given special permission to take part in the Queen's Speech debate but was otherwise advised not to use his voice for as long as possible. This caused much delight in the Kinnock household where he had to pass notes and was unable to shout at his family. But as his great strength, or, his critics would claim, his only strength, was his oratory, loss of speech appeared to be a serious disadvantage to his campaign. However, this seeming disaster was now an asset that assisted his leadership chances. He had got ahead of his competitors largely on the basis of his personal qualities and his proven dedication to Labour. His team now wanted to maintain this lead with a low-profile campaign so that Kinnock would not have to develop specific policies. Without a voice, this was possible; moreover his silence added humour to an otherwise uninteresting campaign, and he got considerable credit as it was appreciated that his voice had been injured during the general election while campaigning for the Labour Party. Although successful on television and at conferences, his performance in the House of Commons had always been modest. The Queen's Speech debate had therefore at first seemed an opportunity to demonstrate his ability as a parliamentarian. Labour MPs crowded into the chamber to hear him: however, when he spoke it was with a scarcely audible croak. As he had nothing to offer in terms of policy, this was just as well: he got great credit for trying and general approval from Labour MPs for his attack on the Tory government. He accused Mrs Thatcher of trying to find motives for economies in the welfare state, and said that the Tory programme had been 'a declaration of war' on the sick and the poor.

Kinnock had to write and have people read for him in his absence speeches that had already been arranged. A performer from 'The

Archers' was hired to deliver a Kinnock speech in Birmingham, at an education, training and development conference. Another important occasion was the Mackintosh Memorial Lecture at Edinburgh University, that he had been asked to give some time previously, and had already written some weeks before the June general election. Since the death of Professor Mackintosh the Labour Party as a whole, and the PLP in particular, had been seriously lacking a worthy ideologue. This was therefore an opportunity for Kinnock to give some intellectual substance to his bid for the leadership. He argued, in the paper that was read for him, that Labour had been declining during the 1970s so the Party would now have drastically to alter its attitudes towards the electorate. He stated that even Trotsky had said, 'It is not enough to create a programme, it is necessary that the working class accept it.' Kinnock argued that the far left were 'so obsessed with ideology that they cannot see the people for the slogans. They prefer the comforts of indignation to the challenges of victory. They reduce politics to the level of a hobby.' Labour, he claimed, would have to learn from its general election defeat. Despite the soundness of his argument, there were several commentators who were disappointed at Kinnock's lack of intellectual substance.

Despite his voice trouble, he continued his public appearances. He was enthusiastically greeted as guest of honour at the fortieth anniversary of Church Street Nursery School, Tredegar, which he himself used to attend. After the meeting he decided to go home to his family in London in his Ford Sierra. Driving along the M4, at 1.45 a.m., his car suddenly swerved violently to the left. Kinnock tried to control it by turning into the skid, but lost control and the car hit a grass verge and somersaulted. Still moving at 70 m.p.h. the wreck overturned several times, careering along on its roof, before halting a hundred yards from the original skid. His thoughts at the time were on trying to control the skid while flying through the air listening to a Brahms tape. When the wreck halted he freed the seat belt which had saved his life and scrambled through a window, thinking, thank God his wife and children hadn't been with him. The car was a total write-off, but although somewhat shaken, Kinnock's only injury was a slightly cut hand. He later said, 'My escape was miraculous'. What amazed onlookers at the time was that he was calm and unruffled, and was even joking and laughing. His main concern appeared to be to find his music tapes. The car accident made Neil Kinnock a household name. Television film crews and journalists besieged the Kinnocks' house in Ealing as Glenys took her husband in her Mini Estate car to the doctor's for a medical check. On television news programmes that evening the accident was the major news story. That Kinnock had been able to survive such a horrific accident did indeed seem miraculous; it enabled him to acquire the aura of charismatic indestructibility which emphasized his image of being a natural winner. So concerned for his health were the trade unions that the TGWU donated him a chauffeur-driven car.

The Kinnock campaign team completed their final survey in July, the findings of which clearly showed that, although this was only the fifth week of a fourteen-week campaign, Kinnock could anticipate getting 75% of the constituency, 60% of the trade union, and 40% of the PLP vote, and thus be certain of winning in October. The team now began, slowly and purposefully, to lessen the electioneering factor, to avoid further damage to the Party, and gradually to project Kinnock as the future leader. Nominations for the leadership closed on 15 July. That week-end Kinnock seemed more than ever the crown prince when, with Glenys, he was televised appearing with Michael Foot at the huge march past during the Durham miners' centenary. That week-end, too, he started a punishing nationwide speaking tour that was to take him to Birmingham, Kent, Manchester, Sheffield, Southampton and Yorkshire.

Meanwhile Kinnock's election manifesto, 'A Summary of Views', was published on 18 July. In this he stated little of substance, other than declaring that Labour's policies were basically sound and did not need altering. However, as he had moved towards pragmatic leadership, he had, during the leadership campaign, found that he needed to dilute his ideas on nuclear disarmament and the Common Market, issues that had been such liabilities at the general election. While maintaining a commitment to unilateral disarmament, he hedged on the matter of Polaris, claiming that by the late 1980s the system would be obsolete. On the Common Market he conceded that withdrawal would no longer be feasible: 'With the prospect of four or five more years of membership, and with Spain and Portugal about to join, the Common Market picture changes.' Instead of withdrawal, he now merely favoured a policy of 'reformism'. Kinnock was thus abandoning one of his most sacred left-wing credentials. He tried to cover his tracks with a considerable amount of meaningless phraseology: 'The Labour Party does not offer policy paralysis but we are determined to get the best for the British people and that will always be the difference between us and Margaret Thatcher however many tantrums she throws.' Surmising that a test for Labour would be the European Assembly elections in June 1984, Kinnock made a much publicized trip to Strasbourg to speak with Labour MEPs.

A significant media event that was to work further to Kinnock's advantage was a televised debate between the four candidates. This was staged by the Fabian Society, and broadcast as a BBC *Newsnight* special programme on 31 July, entitled 'The Labour Leadership Debate'. The candidates had each to speak for five minutes, then answer questions. Kinnock had Glenys watching him in the audience and, looking much younger than his forty-one years, was generally agreed to have made the best speeches. He argued that the Labour vote had been crumbling for years, but it was the Party's civil war that had been the factor largely to blame for the general election defeat. To the delight of the constituencies and most of the unions, but to the incredulity of most of the rest of the British electorate watching, he claimed there was nothing wrong with the policies on which the Labour Party had fought the general election. He said that although the last election was a serious defeat for Labour, the job of the Party was to change the attitude of the voters who did not believe that the Party's policies would be effective, rather than to change the policies, adding that 'the main body of our policies must not be jettisoned', but the policies were too bulky in some cases and too vague and shy in others. 'To those people who believe our policies should be discarded in large part or in whole, I offer the advice of Bernard Shaw, "If your face is dirty, wash it. Don't cut your head off".' He argued the need for the Labour Party to improve its presentation, modernize its administration, and attract and maintain new members. But he also made the pragmatic claim that caused his broad left supporters to shudder, when he warned: 'Of our actions and attitudes, let us realize that we can only defend the have-nots of our country and the world, if we secure the support of the 'haven't-got-enoughs', yes, and in addition, those who 'have enough'. That is not retreat, that is realism. It is not caution, it is calculation. The prerequisite of a serious intention to gain victory for socialism in our country, in our time.'

On the matter of defence policy, he said: 'A nation of our size, capacity and location, needs a defence policy that whilst maintaining full strength of conventional arms and NATO partnership uses Britain's nuclear status for the sole purpose of securing force reductions, culminating in a non-nuclear defence strategy within the lifetime of a Parliament.'

When asked if his previous lack of office was not a disadvantage, he stated:

> If your pre-condition of leadership were experience of similar office, that would deny in most of the countries of the world the possibility of most of the people who seek and secure office from ever becoming leaders of the parties or their countries. Whilst I recognize that the experience of my comrades is of value, I don't think I would consider it to be a pre-condition. I think the qualities that our party should be looking for are common sense, energy, and socialist commitment.

Meanwhile, despite the hope of the Kinnock campaign team that the leadership election would not harm Labour, the Penrith by-election showed that the public was increasingly disenchanted with what it had seen of Labour's internal arguing, and its adherence to its old policies. An election at the Lake District constituency of Penrith had been arranged because of the promotion to Leader of the House of Lords of the Conservative MP for twenty-eight years, William Whitelaw. The Conservatives were defending a comfortable majority of 15,421, from a few weeks earlier when Labour had been in third place with 6,612 votes. The Conservatives won the 28 July Penrith by-election but with a majority that had crumbled to 552. This was entirely because of the SDP candidate who had won 16,978 votes. Labour, with only 2,834 votes, were decimated and lost their deposit. At Penrith in 1979 Labour had achieved 9,984 votes, nearly one-fifth of the electorate; in June 1983, 6,612 votes, 13% of the electorate; and in July only 7.7%. The result was a sensational achievement for the SDP and was hailed as the start of its struggle to oust Labour as the major opposition party. That the heart of the Labour Party itself was at fault and causing people to defect was made clear because the traditional reasons for Labour's defeat no longer seemed to apply. Benn had ceased to be an MP, and Foot was retiring. That this was an unfortunate sign for Labour was further accentuated when on 18 August a Gallup survey showed that the Conservatives had actually increased their lead by 1% since the general election, and the SDP had overtaken Labour as the main opposition party, with 29% of the vote to Labour's mere 25%. If this trend were to continue, there would not be much of a party for Kinnock to lead.

During August campaigning for the candidates slowed and Kinnock was able to take his family on a holiday abroad. On his return he took them to a good-humoured demonstration in London, concerned with a protest against cuts in Government grants to the Arts Council. Sir Harold Wilson's leadership campaign, many years earlier, had cost 1s. 4d., the price of telephoning supporters asking them *not* to campaign for him. While the *Tribune* letters appealing for money had helped with the £1,000 cost of the Kinnock campaign, this had not been enough, so the campaign team had decided to stage a satirical review. This was most successful, and included Kinnock's daughter Rachel strumming a guitar and singing a tune concerning her father. The Brahms tape that had survived Kinnock's car accident was auctioned. This presidential style of campaigning was greatly criticized by the other leadership competitors, but for Kinnock the event, which was televised, made his campaign seem fun, and was a useful electioneering coup.

The increasing theme of his speeches was the need for Party unity. Speaking at a meeting in Wandsworth on 8 September he said that when he was leader the Party would be preparing for 'the long march'. His need to keep the issues simple during the election campaign concealed a certain naïvety on matters of State. When asked to give his views on the statement made in Moscow by the miners' leader Arthur Scargill, that Mrs Thatcher was a 'threat to world peace', Kinnock, speaking on the commercial television programme TV-am, agreed that she was a threat to world stability. When asked whether he considered the Soviet Union a greater threat to Britain than the United States, he said, 'There is an almost miserable equality of threat'. Such comments did Kinnock no harm among the Labour constituency parties, from where he would get the greatest number of votes, but his views were of little consequence to the mass of the British people.

There was an enhancement for Kinnock's campaign on 12 September when the NEC post-mortem on the general election unanimously agreed that the reasons for the catastrophic defeat were nothing to do with Foot's leadership, nor the main policies on which Labour had fought. What criteria the NEC used to arrive at such an incredible conclusion is beyond intelligent comprehension. Opinion polls had consistently shown Foot to be the most unpopular opposition leader ever recorded, and during the election Labour canvassers on the doorstep had unanimously found that the Party's policy of unilateral nuclear disarmament had been the issue which had lost it most support. However, in the tradition of a bad worker blaming his tools, the NEC investigation had found that there was nothing wrong with Labour's policies, but that the defeat had mostly been a matter of organization and presentation. This was what Kinnock had been arguing during the leadership campaign, and thus these NEC findings endorsed his campaign. Speaking at a meeting at Stoke-on-Trent that evening, he launched a ten-point plan for the modernization of the party machinery. Among the reforms were proposals to recruit 250,000 new members, improvements in efficiency at the Walworth Road headquarters, and quality training for party employees, especially agents. He said there should also be a national office with an NEC subcommittee specifically responsible for campaigning. Kinnock had no illusions concerning the need for Labour to have a good public image, especially with the press. He said, 'Labour Party members must know that the Party is permanently on trial by the media and statements by Party members can have major adverse effects.' He argued that if Labour was to be a mass party it would have to be sensible: 'We need an informed, knowledgeable, trained membership which is confident in its ideas and can present them without dogmatizing or browbeating to a public that will ignore the most compelling message if it is delivered arrogantly.' In early September he was able to visit the TUC conference at Blackpool with the sense of being an assured winner. He was able to strengthen personal ties with trade union leaders, advising them to get rid of the unions' militant left-wingers.

As the Labour conference week approached, the Kinnocks were made the subject of intense press interest. Fleet Street had suddenly 'discovered' Glenys Kinnock who, to her horror, found she was hounded by photographers, even when visiting Sainsburys. Profiles of Glenys appeared in newspapers erroneously showing her as a Lady Macbeth who was also an attractive Welsh schoolteacher. The Kinnocks were besieged by the press on arriving at Brighton, and when interviewed with Neil by BBC television Glenys spoke of her apprehension for the family if Kinnock was elected Party leader. On the morning of 2 October, while walking on the beach, the Kinnocks were suddenly trapped by large waves. Kinnock clutched at his wife and pushed her to safety, but lost his balance and fell into the sea. Soaking wet, he told the Press, 'I bet it wouldn't happen to Maggie'.

That afternoon votes were cast for the leadership. During the count, scrutineers confused the proportions of the franchise assigned to the trade unions and the MPS. However, this did not affect Kinnock's overwhelming win. Although confident of winning by an estimated 67%, he waited nervously on the platform, scribbling the numbers as the votes were announced. A late dash of support by MPs had given him an even larger margin than was anticipated. He had achieved 29% of the 40% in the trade union section, 27% of the 30% in the constituencies, and 14% of the 30% in the Parliamentary Party. Of the total franchise, Kinnock had won a massive 71%, Hattersley 19%, Heffer 6%, and Shore 3%. The Conference jumped to its feet, clapping loudly, as Kinnock acknowledged the applause and beckoned Glenys onto the platform. Mistiming her cue, the wife of the new Labour leader found a line through the media, joined her husband, and waving and laughing the Kinnocks acknowledged the applause.

As Neil and Glenys chatted on the platform, attention switched for a time to the battle for the deputy leadership for which a 'knife-edge' result had been anticipated. Meacher had been hoping for the support of the NUM, NUR and TGWU trade unions, but their last-minute decision to support Hattersley and a larger-than-anticipated move for Hattersley among the constituencies, meant that he was comfortably elected deputy leader. The percentages of the votes cast for the deputy leadership were: Hattersley 67%, Meacher 27%, Denzil Davies 3% and Gwyneth Dunwoody 1%. The soft left 'dream ticket' had been achieved, and after Hattersley had dashed to the stage to thunderous applause, Kinnock commenced his winner's speech. Despite the months of campaigning he had, as usual, not written a speech in advance. Although he had a few ideas for what was one of the most important speeches of his career, he had waited until he was at the Conference and had been elected leader before making notes for it. He said:

> What we have proved in this election is that we can have democracy without enmity, a contest without conflict, and that has done us good, and it has built our strength. [loud applause]
>
> Here in this crowded, dangerous, beautiful world there is only hope if there is hope together for all peoples. Our function, our mission, our objective as socialists is to see that we gain the power to achieve that and there is no other way to achieve it but by socialism. Socialism that does not count its greatness in the numbers of warheads it has got ... socialism that would enjoy pride and patriotism; socialism that would ensure that the sick, old, young, and poor have their just share of the wealth of this massively prosperous country. [loud applause]
>
> To get that we have to win. We have to win. And we must be of the people, and for the people. If we want to win ... we have to commend the common sense of socialism, the realism of socialism ... and if anyone wants to know the reasons why we must conduct ourselves in this fashion, just remember ... how you felt on that dreadful morning of June 10th, just remember how you felt then and think to yourselves, June 9th 1983, never, ever, again ... [loud applause]
>
> Show that we understand it, show that we mean it, show we know, taught by the hardest school of events, that unity is the price of victory, not unity four weeks before the next general election, not unity before the local elections next year, but unity here and now, and from henceforth ... but living working unity of people, of a movement, of a party who have a conviction, who want to win in order to save our country and our world.
>
> It is not just that we can win; we will win. [loud applause]

Kinnock's election to the leadership and his speech had set the mood of party unity for the conference. Not stopping for celebrations he immediately made a dash for the television and radio studios. But he was now cautious. Although he emphasized the need for unity, he advocated minimal change. On the BBC he said, 'There are organizational changes that need to be made . . . different deployments of our strength in Parliament that need to be undertaken. There are questions of presentations of our policy that need to be looked at.' Now he was leader, he was having to reconcile the grim realities of the need for the Party to achieve mass support to win general elections with the abstractions of Labour policy. This new caution was nowhere more evident than concerning the matter of defence. Even hours before the leadership election, he had abstained on an NEC nuclear disarmament motion because he did not like the use of the word 'unconditional'. Despite his argument that there should be a reconsideration of the nuclear matter, the NEC approved the motion. This need to produce a coherent defence policy was more noticeable when the Conference voted for resolutions demanding multilateralism and immediate unilateralism. During the defence debate, Callaghan had angrily to defend himself from the claim that he had sabotaged the election campaign. Kinnock took no part in the debate, but miserably listened to it on the platform: it made clear to him the need for Labour to clarify practical and vote-winning policies.

The sense at the Conference was that with a dynamic young leadership things could not get worse for Labour. Yet its isolation from political thinking in the country seemed more evident when the speech of the noble Michael Foot, who had led the Party to its humiliating defeat, was greeted with adoration and acclaim. However, they reserved their greatest enthusiasm for the hero of the week, and heir to the Bevanite tradition, Neil Kinnock, who made his first main conference speech on the subject of the welfare state, the first few pages of which had been written weeks before, but most of which had been scribbled on the platform. He said,

> I thank you for electing me leader of the Labour Party. I thank you . . . for giving me such immense support. . . . It offered me a duty, and it gave me the authority to insist that the single purpose of my leadership will be to advance the cause of Labour and to secure victory for this party. [applause]
> That must be the single cause of not just leadership, but of mem-

bership too. And I want to thank you for accepting that obligation and demonstrating this week that you do accept that obligation of securing victory for Labour.... We have much to do. We have to win elections at every level. We have to recruit. We have to win over a hundred seats just in order to give us a parliamentary majority. It would be a terrible mistake to underestimate the task but it would also be an almost equal mistake to overestimate the task ... in the wake of defeat we build not despondency but determination. And we are going to need all of that determination and coherent persistent unity in order to accomplish the task we have to do....

How does Margaret Thatcher dare to glory in the fact that she is contriving the termination of the welfare state. [loud applause] Because although all of the effects of these economies, so called, are on the real people, they are made by people who don't understand the needs of real people in our country.... [long applause]

I'll tell you a much simpler way of rejuvenating people.... without all the magic of modern medicine. Rejuvenate people by giving them pensions that are capable of meeting heating costs ... rejuvenate them by giving them transport at a price that they can afford and at a frequency that they can depend upon to free them from isolation. Rejuvenate them by giving them medical services to free them from pain.... Rejuvenate them by giving them safe streets to walk on. That's the rejuvenation that we want, and it does mean that we have to be unremitting in our defence of the public services, local government services, health services. That defence of those services is a national duty that doesn't only apply to this movement. I make the appeal to all the people of this country, no matter what they voted on June 9th ... join with us in the defence of a basic, fundamental, essential health service, without which this country ceases to be civilized. [long applause]

Is it efficiency to contrive that for the first time in British history ... this manufacturing, producing, trading nation is actually buying more manufactured goods from abroad than we're selling to the rest of the world? ... It is a grand-scale act of profound economic treachery. That is what they're doing to your country.... We have a 'scorched earth economy' in Britain now because of the way they have been misconducting our affairs.... The people of whom we speak, the people to whom we speak, the British people, have this country as their own, invest their lives in it, want it to be nourished and developed, and I say to them we are the only party with that similar scale of commitment to permit that nourishment to take place....

I've had enough of people who believe we can have serenity in this world when national greatness is measured in war chests, I've had enough of dreamers who think that we can have national pride, national satisfaction when the sick, and the old, and the poor, are ordered to make the major sacrifices to national strength....

We must produce out of slump or we do not get out of slump, realists who know that such production needs investment and demand, or we do not get such recovery. Realists who require efficiency in the use of resources and not the massive costs of the disuse of people and capital. Realists who want rewards for merit instead of privileges for those who inherit.... Realists who understand that patriotism is not an empty clanging replay of the past but the belief in the people of the present and in their potential for the future. Realists who will not accept the delusion of great-power status, or the ruinous risks and costs that go with it. Realists. That is what is needed in this country. The realism of democratic socialism. That is the patriotism that I feel in my blood and in my bones. In my brain and heart I know that is the kind of patriotism that the people of this country really feel. The patriotism of peace, the patriotism of care ... of confidence, yes, and of efficiency, yes. That is today's patriotism and this Labour movement is made up of today's people who borrow nothing from nostalgia, whether for [from] the 1950s and 1960s or 1920s or the 1820s.... And when those who prate about blimpish patriotism in the mode of Margaret Thatcher, are also the ones who will take millions off the caring services of this country, I wonder they don't choke on the very word patriotism. [applause]

They are the enemy, they must be defeated, and we must defeat them together. If we try by groups and factions we won't do it. If we give greater attention to arguments between ourselves than in our enmity against them we won't do it.... They are the enemy, they must be defeated and we must defeat them together. That is our purpose. There must be no activity in this Labour movement that is superior to that purpose.... Let us go to it. [loud applause]

Kinnock's speech was greeted with thunderous applause and a standing ovation, noticeably from each section of the Conference, MPs, constituency parties, and trade unions. His demand for unity had been in tune with an acceptance by the Conference of Labour's need to escape the possibility of obliteration. Press reaction to his speech was cautiously favourable, and it was given special attention as much of the conference proceedings had been overshadowed by the news of the Parkinson scandal. Kinnock's belief in the need for caution was shared by the Party. The Conference by electing a left-wing leader dashed the hopes of the far left in the elections to the NEC, whose composition remained unaltered with a large majority for the centre right. This meant that Kinnock could control the NEC, and the chairmanships of its committees would go to people acceptable to the new leader. The elections for the shadow cabinet also showed little change with a preponderance of moderates. Kinnock also appointed moderates to the most important jobs, with Hattersley as shadow Chancellor, Silkin with the defence portfolio, and Healey as shadow Foreign Secretary. With John Prescott, Michael Meacher, Robin Cook, John Cunningham, and Barry Jones as new appointees, there was surprise that Kinnock had not promoted more younger MPs.

For the Kinnocks the Labour leadership meant a change in living style. Nevertheless Glenys was determined to continue with her teaching job. Kinnock's salary was now £36,000, and he had a chauffeur-driven official car, and a team of special detectives. Although he had formally objected to any form of self-glorification, he now took some pleasure in having his career compared with that of Harold Wilson and John F. Kennedy. During a hectic week his education assistant, Charles Clarke, and his secretary, Maureen Willis, moved his papers to the comfortable suite of parliamentary offices assigned to the Leader of the Opposition. There was, however, soon criticism that the young team with which Kinnock had surrounded himself were mediocrities. However, Kinnock had been determined to improve administration and had sacked a number of the Foot entourage, whom he believed were sycophants and idlers. It was a meritocrat belief of his that people should only be promoted who were of proven worth.

With Kinnock as leader, the Labour Party dramatically increased in popularity in opinion surveys, to the detriment of the SDP. A Harris survey in October 1983 showed that an estimated 42% of people questioned, favoured the Conservatives, 39% Labour and 18% the SDP. The Conservatives' lead of just 3% was the lowest since the Falklands War. However, when people were asked who would make the best Prime Minister, 48% said Mrs Thatcher, but only 24% Kinnock. With his minor Party reforms, Kinnock's priority was to improve Labour's image and he personally took charge of the NEC Campaign Committee. But although he was leader, he had few suggestions for winning the millions of additional votes which were needed if a Labour majority was to be gained. His reaction was fundamentally cautious, and there was much disappointment when at the first Prime Minister's Question Time, he confined himself to criticisms of Government spending economies. There was, however, much patience and help given him by Labour MPs, and he was loudly and enthusiastically cheered during his first major speech as leader, when he made a fierce attack on the Conservatives during a Health Service debate in which he condemned the criminal profits made by private drug companies.

The Labour Party continued to improve its standing in opinion surveys. By December a MORI survey showed Labour's support at 39.5% and the Conservatives' at 40.5%. This was Labour's best showing since the civil war during the summer of 1981, and was confirmation of the success of Kinnock's efforts to form Labour into a credible Party of government.

Conclusion

Kinnock is a bright dynamic character with the common touch. To meet he is cheery, more thoughtful and serious than his public image suggests. During the writing of this book the author was kindly granted an interview at the House of Commons where Kinnock radiated good-natured warmth and natural charm. He was courteous and helpful and in answer to questions talked at great length, using three paragraphs when a sentence would have done. Only when asked about his criticism of the monarchy and his abstentions on defence estimates did he appear cautious.

He can be very careless. In May 1976 he and six other Labour MPs tabled a Commons motion congratulating Liverpool on winning the football championship. However, Kinnock had not read the motion, to which he had signed his name, thoroughly, for it also applauded the fans for their exemplary conduct. When this was brought to his attention he withdrew his name and tabled an amendment instead, condemning the violent behaviour of supporters. In October 1979 he and some others on the Labour left signed a small proclamation about Afghanistan, again without checking it. Later he discovered there were thousands of political prisoners in Afghanistan, and that he had put his name to a proclamation initiated by those supporting Russia's presence there. Nor does he appear to have read thoroughly his 1982 entry in *Who's Who* which claims that he has written a book entitled *As Nye Said*.

One of the reasons which Neil Kinnock provided for his resignation as Foot's PPS in February 1975 was that he wanted to finish a book which he was compiling of Aneurin Bevan's speeches. It was also claimed in profiles of him in a couple of newspapers that he just wanted a few weeks to complete the anthology of Bevanisms that he was writing. Finally, in various editions of *Who's Who* Kinnock stated in his entry that the book had actually been published: in the 1975 edition that it was published in 1975; in 1976 that it was published in 1976; in 1977 that it was published in 1976; in 1978 that it was published in 1977; in 1979 that it was published in 1979; in 1980 that it was published in 1980; and, finally, in the 1982 edition that it had been published under the title *As Nye Said* in 1980. In his 1983 *Who's Who* entry there is no mention at all of the book. Curiously, there appears to be no record of the publication of such a book by Kinnock, no mention in the National Bibliography, no record at the British Museum. Indeed, when the author asked Kinnock's literary agent where this published book was to be found, she stated that as far as she knew Kinnock had not even put down a word of it.

When the author asked Kinnock personally where this alleged publication on Bevan's speeches was, he replied:

It's, er, in four cardboard boxes, in the attic at the moment, having been moved there from the garage. Er, I just haven't had the time to finish it off. Its been in existence like that since 1975. I'm not sure how, er, it got in. It started off in *Who's Who* some time ago but, er, you know, frankly, to tell you the truth, its not the kind of thing I give much attention to.

It seems most likely that Kinnock's *Who's Who* references to the book were essentially due to his carelessness. An attempt to make ungenuine claims would not be in accordance with his character which is decent, honest and unassuming. Indeed a significant characteristic of Kinnock's is a detestation of pomp and a good natured ability to laugh at himself.

Ebullient, jovial, talkative, of sound intelligence, he has undoubted charisma and his leadership has brought an immediate and dramatic improvement in the fortunes of the Labour Party. There must however be some cautious scepticism as to whether this will be sufficient to win a general election, especially at a time when a significant reason for Labour's demise is its image of a party of talkers who do not bother to listen. Although revered for his proficiency as a wordsmith, Kinnock is likely to find that as people grow more used to him the novelty of his speaking talents will be a diminishing asset. It is a fatal underestimate of the intelligence of the British electorate to assume that his verbosity will be sufficient to win power for Labour.

Despite Kinnock's lack of experience of government office, he has been hard working and lucky in his career as an MP; he has also had the good fortune to begin his time as Party leader by criticizing the Conservatives where they were most vulnerable, for their conduct of the welfare state, the subject on which he had· most knowledge. However intense the feeling within the Labour Party for the Health Service, and for unilateral nuclear disarmament, these are the old-fashioned Bevanite obsessions of the 1950s, shibboleths from which Labour will have to free itself if it is to begin to have a chance of winning another general election. Indeed, fundamental to the decline of the Labour Party has been a mood, of which Kinnock will have to rid the Party, of sheer arrogant pseudo-intellectual contempt for the British electorate. Kinnock's own interests are narrow and seem confined to Welsh affairs, coal mining, steel problems and the welfare state. He knows very little about finance. He drew attention to his lack of knowledge of such matters in a previously unnoticed speech in the House of Commons on 4 April 1978, stating that 'other than when playing darts, I become confused at the mere mention of figures'. He also lacks experience of ministerial office, which means that he might not have the breadth of vision over the whole range of government activities needed to provide confidence to win the necessary millions of votes. His only job of executive responsibility has been that of president of the Students' Union at Cardiff University. He has cautiously taken steps to broaden his image: in 1984 he visited Greece and the United States and he has plans to visit the Soviet Union. However, there must be genuine doubt as to whether his programmes and determination to improve the lot of the working people will not, if put into practice, lead to falling standards for the vast mass of British middle-class people.

Kinnock's reputation for scheming Machiavellian ambition is undeserved: in fact his career shows a surprising lack of calculation. His hazardous defiance of his party on Welsh devolution indeed showed a disregard of the consequences and great personal courage. His intense dedication to the Labour Party is unsurpassed, and as a parliamentary debater he has revitalized the morale of the Parliamentary Labour Party. Kinnock knows that he is the only Labour left-wing politician of his generation who can win votes and laughs from the general public, and as a popular and formidable leader he is indispensable to the Party. He is a gifted meritocrat who has succeeded by natural ability and hard work, but he believes that he should lead by example and considers that Labour MPs should work as hard for the Labour Party as he has undoubtedly done. There does however seem to be a significant belief that whatever is good for Neil Kinnock is also good for the Labour Party and this, with his centralist views of government, hints at headstrong leadership.

While a superb Party leader, what Kinnock lacks is credibility. Apart from his undoubted ability to charm the public, much of his usefulness rests on his power to win votes. However, for the Labour Party this could be a dangerous myth. The historical evidence clearly suggests that while Kinnock can enthuse audiences with his speeches and can encourage Labour voters at public meetings, he has never won votes other than from committed Labour supporters. At the 1983 general election his Falklands speeches meant he was a vote *loser* for Labour, and his education policy was a disappointment that was rejected by parents, teachers, and the unemployed, precisely those voters for whom he believed it had been designed. His determined stand over unilateral disarmament is also a vote loser.

Kinnock's success story is one of the most remarkable in British political history. He commands the trust of the Party and has the personality to be a great Labour leader. He is one of the most pleasant characters on the modern political scene, has natural powers of leadership, pragmatism and patriotism, but were Labour to win another general election there is some fear that he might prove to be just a talented MP, lacking the breadth of mind or the temperament to be a Prime Minister. Were he to lead a government, he might find himself defeated by an old law of politics: it is one thing to take power, but quite another to keep it.

Bibliography

Journals

The Economist; Education; Labour Monthly; Labour Weekly; Marxism Today; The Miner; New Socialist; The Teacher; Times Educational Supplement; Times Higher Educational Supplement; Political Quarterly.

Newspapers

Daily Mirror; Daily Telegraph; Evening Standard; Financial Times; Guardian; Morning Star; News of the World; Observer; South Wales Echo; Star; Sun; Sunday Express; Sunday Telegraph; Sunday Times; The Times; Tribune; Western Mail.

Works by Neil Kinnock

General Election Leaflets (Bedwellty Labour Party) 1970, 1979, 1983
'Wales and the Common Market', 1971
Foreword to A. Bevan, *In Place of Fear* (Quartet, London), reissued 1978
'Facts to Beat the Fantasies', Labour, No Assembly Campaign, Wales (mimeographed), February 1979
'Education for the Twenty-first Century', Chapter 7 of G. Kaufman, ed., *Renewal: Labour's Britain in the 1980s* (Penguin, Harmondsworth), 1983
'John P. Mackintosh Memorial Lecture', University of Edinburgh (mimeographed), 24 June 1983
'A Summary of Views – Neil Kinnock MP', Kinnock Leadership Campaign, House of Commons (mimeographed), July 1983
With N. Butler and T. Harris, *Why Vote Labour?* (NCLC Publishing Society, London), April 1979
With P. Coyte, 'How to Speak in Public' (Labour Party, London), 1980
With R. Hattersley, E. Heffer and P. Shore *Labour's Choices*, Fabian Tract 489 (Fabian Society, London), July 1983

Bibliography

Other publications

V. Brome, *Aneurin Bevan* (Longman, Green & Co.: London), 1953

B. Castle, *The Castle Diaries 1974–76* (Weidenfeld & Nicolson: London), 1980

H. Davies and F. Hermann, *Great Britain, a celebration* (Hamish Hamilton: London), 1982

Hansard, 1970–83

S. Haseler, *The Tragedy of Labour* (Basil Blackwell: Oxford), 1980

R. Hattersley, 'A Duty to Win' (mimeographed), House of Commons, July 1983

T. Herald, *Networks* (Hodder & Stoughton: London), 1983

S. Hoggart and D. Leigh, *Michael Foot: a portrait* (Hodder & Stoughton: London), 1981

P. Keller and C. Hitchens, *Callaghan: The Road to Number Ten* (Cassell: London), 1976

M.M. Krug, *Aneurin Bevan: Cautious Rebel* (Thomas Yoseoff: New York), 1961

D. Kogan and M. Kogan, *The Battle for the Labour Party* (Kogan Page: London), 1982

Labour Party, '16–19 Learning for Life', 1982
    'Labour's Programme', 1982
    'The New Hope for Britain', Labour's Manifesto 1983

A. Mitchell, *Four Years in the Death of the Labour Party* (Methuen: London), 1983

H. Pelling, *A Short History of the Labour Party* (Macmillan: London), 7th edn, 1982

L. Smith, *Harold Wilson: The Authentic Portrait* (Hodder & Stoughton: London), 1964

M. Stewart, *Politics and Economic Policy in the UK since 1964* (Pergamon Press: London), 1978

Harold Wilson, *Final Term: The Labour Government 1974–1976* (Weidenfeld & Nicolson: London), 1979

Workers' Educational Association, South Wales District, *Annual reports*, 1966–70, *75 Years of Service*, 1982

Acronyms

AEUW	Amalgamated Union of Engineering Workers
ASLEF	Associated Society of Locomotive Engineers and Firemen
ASTMS	Association of Scientific, Technical and Managerial Staffs
BBC	British Broadcasting Corporation
CBI	Confederation of British Industry
CLPD	Campaign for Labour Party Democracy
CND	Campaign for Nuclear Disarmament
COHSE	Confederation of Health Service Employees
EEC	European Economic Community
EEPTU	Electrical, Electronic, Telecommunication and Plumbing Union
IMF	International Monetary Fund
ITN	Independent Television News
LCC	Labour Co-ordinating Committee
NCLC	National Council of Labour Colleges
NEC	National Executive Committee
NUM	National Union of Mineworkers
NUPE	National Union of Public Employees
NUR	National Union of Railwaymen
NUS	National Union of Students
NUT	National Union of Teachers
SDP	Social Democratic Party
SEA	Socialist Educational Association
SNP	Scottish Nationalist Party
PLP	Parliamentary Labour Party
PPS	Parliamentary Private Secretary
SOGAT	Society of Graphical and Allied Trades

TGWU	Transport and General Workers' Union
TLV	Trade Unions for a Labour Victory
TUC	Trades Union Congress
TVS	Television South
UCW	Union of Communication Workers
USDAW	Union of Shop, Distributive and Allied Workers
WEA	Workers' Educational Association

Index